Black Studies Programs
in Public Schools

Raymond H. Giles, Jr.

The Praeger Special Studies program—utilizing the most modern and efficient book production techniques and a selective worldwide distribution network—makes available to the academic, government, and business communities significant, timely research in U.S. and international economic, social, and political development.

ESEA
TITLE-II GRANT

Black Studies Programs in Public Schools

PRAEGER SPECIAL STUDIES IN U.S. ECONOMIC, SOCIAL, AND POLITICAL ISSUES

Praeger Publishers   New York   Washington   London

Framingham State College
Framingham, Massachusetts

Library of Congress Cataloging in Publication Data

Giles, Raymond H.
    Black studies programs in public schools.

    (Praeger special studies in U. S. economic,
social, and political issues)
    Bibliography: p.
    1. Afro-American studies—United States.
I. Title.
E184. 7. G54   917. 3'06'96073   73-3675

PRAEGER PUBLISHERS
111 Fourth Avenue, New York, N.Y. 10003, U.S.A.
5, Cromwell Place, London SW7 2JL, England

Published in the United States of America in 1974
by Praeger Publishers, Inc.

Printed in the United States of America

CONTE

Page

Chapter

Black Studies Programs in Public Schools

CULTURAL DIVERSITY AND THE AMERICAN
PUBLIC SCHOOLS

> Our nation is moving toward two societies, one white, one
> black—separate and unequal. . . . The most fundamental
> [cause of the riots] is the racial attitude and behavior of
> white Americans toward black Americans. . . . Race and
> prejudice has shaped our history decisively; it now threat-
> ens to affect our future. . . . White racism is essentially
> responsible for the explosive mixture which has been
> accumulating in our cities since the end of World War II.[1]

This was the conclusion drawn by the National Advisory Committee on Civil Disorders appointed by President Johnson in 1968.
The significance of this statement is the fact that for the first time
in the history of the United States an official government agency traced
the cause of civil disturbances to the fact that the United States was
a racist society.

This study was conducted with the belief that to a large extent
the problem of racial prejudice and discrimination can and should be
addressed through the schools for several reasons. First, the school
is a social agency that is expected, and claims, to reflect and deal
with current and critical issues that affect and influence our society
and culture. Secondly, one of the major functions of any educational
system is the selection and preservation of selected traditions and
culture. Finally, if the American people want to preserve and realize
more fully, as James Quillen suggests, then the schools should be
considered to have a major responsibility in helping all children
develop racial attitudes that are consistent with democratic ideals.

To what extent is this being attempted, and if so, how, were the questions this study was designed to address. This examination and analysis of ethnic and minority studies programs in the elementary and secondary schools was undertaken with the belief that ethnically oriented programs, related to curricula reform and designed to encourage desired attitudes and values, can be developed within the framework of the existing institutional structure of the American educational system; and that such programs should be developed and be considered consistent with the already stated goals of that system. This premise further assumes the sincerity and commitment of the American public school systems to end racism in the schools by developing the concept that the society in which we live is multi-ethnic, that similarities and differences are a basic condition of American life, that the individuals in our society have as a resource ethnicity as a basis for the realization of self-worth, and that the school as an educational institution is the appropriate vehicle for the realization and affirmation of these principles. Based on the above assumptions, the study proceeded to examine the impact of existing programs in black studies and the kinds of problems that have resulted from the attempts of twenty-five major school districts throughout the United States to develop effective strategies in relation to these and other goals.

PREVAILING AMERICAN ATTITUDES TOWARD
HISTORY OF BLACK PEOPLE IN THE
UNITED STATES

In the summer of 1968, the Opinion Research Corporation made a survey of racial attitudes of a representative sample of Americans for CBS news. One of the questions asked the respondents was: "Would you say that Negroes (blacks) have played an important part or not a very important part in the history of this country?" These were the results:

	Black	White
Important	80%	52%
Not Important	5	32
No Opinion	15	16

Whites had mixed reasons for thinking the Negroes important in our history:
"We learned about Booker T. Washington and some others in school, and there must be lots of others we don't know about."
"Well, they are willing to fight for the country. There are probably other things, but I can't think of any right now."

"They are starting a war right now. They, like Bunche, Jackie
Robinson, and Paul Robson [sic], are out for all they can get. They
want to be important and will riot to make it."

"We gave them everything they have today. They always got
everything for nothing; now they expect it."

The 32 percent who thought that blacks were unimportant justified
their opinions in ingenious ways:

"Well, there's no colored person in the government. I don't
know what other reason I could give."

"All you hear about is Uncle Tom's Cabin and Black Sambo and
those kinds of things. They are just here and we're stuck with them.
They don't do much of anything."

"Reading and studying shows that very little has been given by
the Negro race."

"They haven't had a chance to play an important part."

"They are important for nothing but prize fighting."

"I have had contact with some who steal. As a result, I feel that
since they cannot be trusted, they cannot play a prominent part in
making worthwhile decisions."

By contrast, listen to one black man, who spoke for many of the
80 percent of blacks who believed that their people made important
history:

"We're part of the society. We dug the ditches, planted the cotton.
We've played a big part."

Attitudes such as these have led many educators to conclude that
the way American history has been taught in the public schools is
largely responsible for such widely held views regarding the role of
black people and other nonwhite minorities.

THE TREND TOWARD ETHNIC AND CULTURAL
HERITAGE PROGRAMS

In February, March, and May 1970, hearings were conducted
before the General Subcommittee on Education of the Committee on
Education and Labor in the House of Representatives, Ninety-First
Congress, Second Session on a bill (H.R. 14910) that would provide
a program to improve the opportunity for students in elementary and
secondary schools to study cultural heritages of the major ethnic
groups in the nation.

Congressman Roman Pucinski, Chairman of the Subcommittee,
opened the hearing with the following remarks:

The Nation's youth are engrossed in a restless, sometimes
tumultuous, and often threatening search for identity. Our

young people want to know who they are, where they belong, how they can remain distinctive: special individuals amidst the pervasive pressure for conformity.

This important legislative proposal recognizes a two-fold purpose: First, that American youth should have the opportunity to study, in depth, about their own ethnic backgrounds—about the rich traditions of their forefathers in the arts and humanities, languages and folklore, natural and social sciences—and the many ways in which these past generations have contributed to American life and culture.

A second and equally vital purpose of the Bill is to create greater awareness and appreciate the multi-ethnic composition of our society through a broadly based study of the readily identifiable ethnic groups in our Nation.[2]

Representative Pucinski's statement suggests a set of educational goals related to all ethnic studies programs and provides a rationale common to the interest of all Americans. Although this proposed legislation came at a time when increased pride and dignity had already prompted many black Americans to demand an interpretation of the American past that did justice to the black presence, the expressed need for ethnic studies programs by the United States Congress transcended the concerns of black people and presented the ethnically biased American public school curriculum as an American problem rather than a uniquely black problem. In commenting on the "melting pot" approach, which the schools have advocated until recently to the ethnic variety present in American society, Congressman Pucinski concludes:

Experience has taught us that the pressure toward homogeneity has been superficial and counterproductive; that the spirit of ethnicity, now lying dormant in our national soul, begs for reawakening in a time of fundamental national need.

There are some who would question the value of studying about differences among human groups—about the ways in which we are culturally unique and in a sense separate from one another. But they overlook the basic fact that diversity has brought strength to our Nation; that differences, when understood and valued, can unite disparate groups.[3]

Although the need for ethnic studies programs has been described in the words of the Congressman as "national," nowhere is this need more vocally expressed than among black Americans. This vocalness explains, in part, why in many school districts black, Afro-American, or African studies are being introduced for both black and white children.

PROSPECTS FOR MAJOR CURRICULA REVISION AND PROBLEMS RELATED TO THE PLACEMENT OF BLACK STUDIES INTO THE REGULAR SCHOOL PROGRAM

In April 1971, the Senate Committee on Labor and Public Welfare recommended passage of a bill: Emergency School Aid and Quality Integrated Education. Part of the purpose of the bill was:

(1) to assist school districts to meet special problems incident to desegregation, and to the elimination, reduction, or prevention of minority group isolation in elementary and secondary schools.

(2) to provide financial assistance for the establishment and maintenance of stable, quality, integrated education in elementary and secondary schools and to assist school districts to overcome the adverse educational effects of minority group isolation.[4]

The amount of $500 million was authorized for the period ending June 30, 1972, and $1 billion for fiscal year 1973.

To be eligible, a local education agency must adopt a comprehensive district-wide plan for the elimination of minority group isolation to the maximum extent possible in all its schools. It must also establish or maintain at least one stable, quality, integrated school which contains a substantial proportion of children from educationally advantaged backgrounds, which is substantially representative of the minority group and non-minority group student population of the school district, and which has an integrated faculty.[5]

In recommending the bill for passage the House Committee went on record as agreeing with the responses of Secretary of Health, Education and Welfare, Elliot Richardson, to an inquiry regarding the policies and educational objectives of the Federal Government:

Every major report or research project dealing with educational problems, indeed, of the disadvantaged children, has concluded that educational development, that is, learning, is greatly hindered by a homogeneous learning environment.

Children learn more from each other than from any other resources of the educational environment.

To create and perpetuate homogeneity is to break and reduce the pool of experience, ideas and values from which other children can draw and contribute to inter-action with other children.

In a heterogeneous environment, cultural diversity can be presented in exciting, interaction, awareness and growth processes, which is education in its truest sense.

New curricula and instructional methods to support a program of integrated instruction, including instruction in language and cultural heritage of minority groups.[6]

One of the elements the committee found particularly important to the success of quality integrated education was that "children with differing languages and cultures must be allowed to learn and respect the language and culture associated with the group to which they belong. All children will benefit from an opportunity to learn about the diverse cultural heritage of their classmates." What is important to note is that the Federal Government, after reviewing the situation, actually took the initiative of not only recommending the integration of blacks into the public school systems but into the curriculum as well. The motivation underlying this apparent attempt at educational reform has been interpreted skeptically by many persons who have reviewed it. Paul M. Sweezey, Marxist economist, in commenting on the role of the Federal Government in educational reform, indicates such Congressional reform measures are no panacea.

The national ruling class has traditionally had little or no economic stake in the ghetto but is seriously concerned about its becoming a focus of social instability and rebellion. The national ruling class is therefore prepared to promote programs, including educational reforms, calculated to pacify the ghetto and reduce the danger which it represents to order and security. The way it tries to do this is through federally designed and financed programs such as the Model Cities program. The trouble is that, given the U.S. Governmental structure, the execution of these programs is the responsibility of the local ruling classes, which of course refuse to cooperate except to the extent that they find it in their interest to do so. The consequence is that these federal programs tend to be aborted or distorted in application and to bring little if any benefit to those they are intended to help.[7]

Operating on the premise that the public schools are the major purveyors of American traditions and cultures and therefore that racial prejudice and discrimination should be addressed through the educational system, this study examined the operation of various ethnic and black studies programs and their impact on racial attitudes. The major purpose of the study was to collect data and information related to the assessment and improvement of these programs in order to propose new strategies and more relevant content and approaches for in-service teacher education programs, establish new projects in the public schools, and evaluate the impact and effectiveness of such programs.

A review of curriculum guides developed by school districts that followed one of the two philosophies operative in the black studies field, separate courses versus curricular revision, was followed by a survey of three elementary school African heritage classes in a predominantly black school district in Harlem. Students were given an open-ended written questionnaire to determine their impressions of the attitudes toward Africa after nine months of studying Africa in a heritage program. Excerpts from taped interviews and discussions with three classes are included for an in-depth look at the attitudes underlying the written responses.

At the secondary level a survey of twenty-five school districts throughout the country with Afro-American studies programs was made, and eight representative case studies were isolated and presented in detail. These case studies include separate black studies courses for black students only in both traditional and experimental predominantly white schools, separate courses in minority studies for white students, required black history courses in all-black high schools, integration of black studies into the regular school curriculum in all-black high schools serving a ghetto, black studies programs in predominantly black high schools serving a middle-class black community, a white teacher of black history in an all-black high school, and a case where a book used to teach black studies in an all-white school district was considered obscene and was removed from the school library by the local police department after a complaint by parents. Each of these case studies examines and presents factors that relate to the strengths and weaknesses of programs in each situation with the aim of providing insights to help administrators consider problems that might arise from similar situations as they attempt to establish such programs.

The curriculum guides from sixteen school districts were analyzed in depth to better understand how those districts suggest black studies be handled. Contributionism, black identity, and a thematic approach emerged as three distinct approaches to the teaching of black studies. Again both the fallacies and strengths of each approach are explored within the educational setting and as they relate to the stated goals of each programs. It was further found that the guides

7

as they exist are not often used in practice. The curriculum guides were also measured against the expressed needs and interests of black students where such needs were openly stated. It was found that the needs of the black community are infrequently considered or understood by persons responsible for the development of course outlines.

The problems of assigning black teachers to teach black studies regardless of their training and the use of black teachers to counsel black students in predominantly white schools is discussed.

The study raises a number of questions calling for varied interpretations and definitions of black studies (each equally valid) and a look at the origin and sponsorship of black studies programs, at the need for clarifying their purposes within diverse settings, at who should teach and who should take black studies, and at the necessity of broader representation of interests and student needs in the development of each program. Much of the solution is seen to be in teacher preparation. Curriculum reform and adequate evaluation techniques for measuring the impact and effectiveness of black studies programs are also discussed, as well as alternatives to the educational problems for which black studies are considered a panacea.

EDUCATIONAL GOALS AND PURPOSES OF ETHNIC AND BLACK STUDIES PROGRAMS

A brief review of the goals expressed in twenty-five curriculum guides developed and distributed by the school districts surveyed reveals a stated aim of seeking to change the black American general image, which is largely considered by both white and black students to be negative as a result of the negative portrayal or omission of blacks from school texts. Most of the developed materials indicate a presumption on the part of most school officials that merely an awareness of black people's contributions to and participation in the progress and development of America will undo the effect created by the failure to mention the black in American history until this time. However, another possibility exists: that biased attitudes toward black people among white teachers and students are not based on ignorance of black achievements or history, thus increased knowledge of the contributions of black people to America would not necessarily result in changed attitudes. From a purely educational standpoint, there is no reason to assume that more knowledge will change attitudes unless the information about minorities is presented in such a way as to create desired impressions.

In many school districts the purpose of introducing black studies is merely to present a more accurate version of American history by including the previously omitted role of a substantial minority group. On the other hand, the stated aims of guides developed by certain districts reveal that the teaching of black history is viewed as a means—the end frequently being an expected change in attitude or behavior on the part of white and black students alike.

Thus, the curriculum guides of most school districts state at least one, sometimes two general aims to justify or explain the reason for black studies. On the other hand, the black population in many school districts has been very outspoken in asserting its demands for separate courses in black studies that will address the need among black children for pride and identity, yet will still remain mindful of the need to remedy the omission of black achievement in the regular school curriculum. The attempt to help black children develop a more positive self- and racial image often results in a compromise between black spokesmen for black community-based schools and white administrators and school board members whose primary concern is apparently the content and quality of education in the predominantly white schools. Since black studies programs can be said to have two separate arms or goals, in many cases two separate approaches take place—curricula reform or revision on the one hand and development of separate courses in black studies for black students on the other.

School administrators in favor of either one of the above approaches can also clearly understand the need felt by many black persons for both. The problem of a racially biased interpretation of American history is not addressed when black studies courses are introduced separately as electives or requirements, or as a series of courses in the form of a program. Indeed, black studies courses introduced into the regular school program at the elementary and secondary school level can do but little to address the biased presentation of American history that led to the need for black studies. The net aim of introducing black studies in many school districts seems to be one of pacifying agitators or militant advocates of black studies who are less concerned with reforming public education than they are with a more immediate problem, namely, the negative effects on their children of a racially biased curriculum. The introduction of black studies in situations where no corresponding attempt at general curricula revision has been made is often, in effect, a trade-off to the black community. Quite often the resulting response among members of the black community has been a tendency to ignore the content of educational programs in predominantly white schools or even schools outside their immediate district or vicinity. For example, in several of the districts visited, black studies was only taught in the high schools that had a significant percentage of black students. In some districts where there were very few or no black students, there were no courses or programs in black history or black studies. The determination of black parents to control the content of the curriculum in predominantly black schools by forcing the inclusion of black studies is often matched only by the resistance to such courses by white parents and administrators who see no need for black studies in predominantly white schools.

Another category of parents is comprised of concerned members of various ethnic and racial groups who feel that there should be only one American history and that it should include the contributions of all groups and thus eliminate the need for separate courses in minority studies to compensate for the omissions. Yet among many persons in this group is an awareness of the academic validity of separate courses in minority studies, as electives, for in-depth study of the society or culture of ethnic minorities. However, the experience of most schools that have introduced black studies courses and programs during the past several years forces one to raise the question, even among those sincerely committed to minority studies or separate courses in black studies, as to whether the public school as it presently exists is an appropriate place for such courses. This concern is based largely on an awareness of the inadequate training, poor preparation, and lack of commitment to the development and supervision of such courses by qualified personnel. Many persons in this latter category feel it is imperative that American history and social studies teachers be expected to be knowledgeable of the interwoven histories, group interaction, development, and common destiny of all groups that comprise the American societal reality.

PHILOSOPHIES, RATIONALES, AND ASSUMPTIONS UNDERLYING GOALS

Black history is viewed in most public schools as a reaction to social or political pressure rather than a valid response to an academic or curricular deficiency. Perhaps that is why the colleges and universities, which are responsible for the training of teachers, do not require them to have a knowledge of the black experience and do not include topics in the black experience in college English, history, or other social science courses required for certification. At present a knowledge of the contributions to history and the culture of black people is not considered necessary for certification either as a requirement of the colleges or of the state departments of education, which determine teacher certification. The department of black or Afro-American studies on most college and university campuses across the country is an undergraduate department offering courses that teachers might find helpful. Such courses are not available on the graduate level for teachers already in service working toward promotion or salary increment. The black studies department, on the other hand, is, in many cases, concerned with problems related to its internal organization, administration, development, and direction and has had little opportunity to examine its potential role as teacher educator for in-service or pre-service programs. There is virtually no cooperation on most college or university campuses between the departments of black studies, where they exist, and the departments of education, which have the responsibility for training teachers. Black studies programs on many campuses are not full departments, as are education, mathematics, French, sociology, and so on, but rather an interdepartmental major or program consisting of a sequence of courses. There is actually less concern voiced for the integration of black studies into the regular school curriculum in the colleges than there is at the public school level. Colleges are seemingly less concerned with the development of positive attitudes and self-images than are the public schools.

What seems to emerge from a general overview of the situation is an indication that many schools have not established black and ethnic studies programs as a response to a felt need for integral curricula reform. On the contrary, black studies programs seem to have been implemented in response to demands from the local community and political pressures outside the community to which school administrators feel compelled to respond. The absence of long-range planning or well-established goals resulting from this situation frequently means that neither the administration nor the faculty is necessarily committed or prepared to undertake a responsibility such as the one that is apparently being forced upon them. This being the situation, there is obviously a need for a clearer and more precise understanding of what the goals of ethnic studies are and how the organization and placement of programs and courses of study are related to the successful achievement of those goals.

A REVIEW OF LITERATURE ON THE VARIOUS APPROACHES TO BLACK STUDIES

This last section will consider selected references bearing on the purposes, goals, and objectives of black studies programs at public schools.

The purpose of black history and black studies has been the topic of many articles, essays, and books during the past seventy-five years. The arguments for and against have led to speculation over the academic validity of such a history by many historians and scholars, both black and white. I will review some of the basic premises underlying the development of programs to teach black history as advanced by black scholars who feel there is a need for black studies but who are equally concerned with defining the purpose.

11

In his book <u>Black Historians: A Critique</u>,[8] Earl Thorpe under-
takes an analysis and interpretation of the black historians and the
histories they have written. Although he is critical of the way in which
some black historians have handled the approach to relating the black
experience, he is of the opinion that black history is needed for at
least three basic reasons: First, (he feels that) American history
has been slow in shedding its aristocratic tradition and bias, which
has been almost exclusively concerned with the affairs of the ruling
class or the elite. This has resulted in blacks and other groups just
being left out. Second, Dr. Carter G. Woodson and other prominent
black scholars who founded the Association for the Study of Negro
Life and History in 1915 felt a need then to combat racial prejudice
and stereotypes. Negative images of black people were a direct result
of very articulate and influential white historians and social scientists
justifying the black man's degraded position in America based on his
biological inferiority. Even today many textbooks depict black people
as emotional, impulsive, nonrational, and lower than average in intel-
ligence and scholastic aptitude. Thus, even today, many educators
justify the need for programs and courses in black studies to correct
this distorted image, which is still being perpetuated by the entertainment media and other American institutions that influence public
opinion.
     A report presented to the California State Board of Education
by members of the History Department at the University of California
at Berkeley contained the following comments concerning specific
United States history textbooks being used in California public schools:
     "The undersigned, American historians and members of the
History Department of the University of California, Berkeley, have
been asked to review the American history textbooks that are most
widely used in California from the standpoint of their treatment of
Negroes. Attached are individual reports on the two state-adopted
textbooks used in grade five, the three state-adopted textbooks used
in grade eight, and the two high school textbooks reported to be most
widely used in the state. These reports disclose an unhealthy condition in California education.
     "In the late nineteenth-century mood of national reconciliation,
based on a widespread assumption of racial superiority among whites
in both North and South, the "southern" view tended to prevail; and
the deference of textbook publishers to the special sensitivities of the
southern market has caused it to continue by and large to prevail in
textbooks until this day. . . . Most of the textbooks we have examined
reflect views on racial and sectional themes that have been rejected
or drastically modified by the best of current historical scholarship.
     "We are additionally concerned <u>as citizens</u> because these his-
torical distortions help perpetuate and intensify the pattern of racial

discrimination which is one of our society's most serious problems. We are concerned not only because much of the material in these books is bad history, but additionally because it is a kind of bad history that reinforces notions among whites of their superiority and among Negroes of their inferiority.

". . . There should be a conscious effort to portray outstanding Negro figures selected by the same criterion of historical significance applied to non-Negro figures. Even these textbooks that now make some effort in this direction tend to single out men like Booker T. Washington and the minor scientist, George Washington Carver, whose attitudes about race relations are least disturbing to conservative whites. Equally or more worthy of inclusion by the standard of historical relevance are men like Denmark Vesey, Nat Turner, Frederick Douglass, W. E. B. DuBois, and the Rev. Martin Luther King.

". . . In the light of these general principles, the greatest defect in the textbooks we have examined is the virtual omission of the Negro. As several of the individual reports point out, the Negro does not "exist" in the books. The authors of the books must know that there are Negroes in America, and have been since 1619, but they evidently do not care to mention them too frequently. In one book there is no account of slavery in the colonial period; in a second, there is not a single word about Negroes after the Civil War; in a third (composed of documents and substantive chapters), the narrative does not mention Negroes in any connection.

". . . All the texts play down or ignore the long history of violence between Negroes and whites, suggesting in different ways that racial contacts have been distinguished by a progressive harmony. The tone of a textbook is almost as important as anything it has to say. In their blandness of amoral optimism these books implicitly deny the obvious deprivations suffered by Negroes. In several places they go further, implying approval for the repression of Negroes or patronizing them as being unqualified for life in a free society."[9]

The above statements indicate only a few of the concerns of American historians about the way blacks have been portrayed. Much more has been said and written on this very important aspect of black studies.

A third reason given by Thorpe to explain the rise of the black history movement in the early 1900s is the need to inspire blacks to high achievement. Thorpe states that people have always sought to inspire the young by telling them of the outstanding qualities of their ancestors. This last reason helps to explain why most of the books published during the early period of the black history movement, up until 1920, were largely biographies of outstanding black persons.

In an article entitled "Rethinking Black History."[10] Dr. Orlando Patterson, professor of Sociology at Harvard, elaborates on the strong emphases placed on black history, both as an end in itself and as a means toward attaining critical psychological, cultural, and political goals.

In Patterson's opinion the major difference between white American history and black American history is that the former concerns itself not so much with an elite and white people as with a literate people, while the latter must concern itself with a people who are not so much lower class and black as preliterate and nonliterate. Thus Patterson's interpretation of black history is radically different from white history, not only in terms of content, but also in technique and method.

He rejects white America's traditional concern for the nation-state and great personalities as a format for presenting a meaningful American Black history; he favors focussing on the black people as a group, on their conditions under an oppressive white society, and, finally, on their patterns of adaptation and techniques for surviving with dignity, which serve, he suggests, as an eloquent testimonial to their resilience. From a different value orientation, Patterson proposes, this might be considered a story of pride and success.

Finally, since the two terms "black history" and "black pride" so often go together, and since the main audience of the black historian demands of him that his works serve not only intellectual but political and moral ends, a word on the relationship between black history and black pride is necessary.

Frazier, in The Black Bourgeoisie,[11] analyzes the frustrations and insecurities of middle-class black Americans in the 1940s, whom he described as isolated, resulting from their rejection by the "white world" and their break with their own cultural traditions. In Frazier's opinion their isolation has resulted in a collective inferiority complex, which has led to their creating a world of make-believe, centered around myths of "Negro business and Negro society." How does an American history teacher fit such a dismal theme into an otherwise national picture of progress and success? Earl Thorpe suggests that until very recently there was never any concern or attempt to understand this problem.

> Black history is that American history, which, until the
> 1960's, was viewed by white America with contempt and
> disdain or ignored altogether, just as black people them-
> selves were viewed and treated. Men tend either to deny
> or force out of consciousness the evil that they do. Much
> of black history, then, is the story of the cruelties and
> inhumanities which a powerful white majority has inflicted
> on a defenseless black minority.[12]

William L. Katz states the case for the need to revise American history in his book Teacher's Guide to American Negro History.[13] Katz quotes the following passage from a northern textbook, which viewed the slave as follows:

As for Sambo, whose wrongs moved the abolitionists to wrath and tears, there is some reason to believe that he suffered less than any other class in the South from its peculiar institution. The majority of the slaves were adequately fed, well cared for, and apparently happy. . . . Although brought to America by force, the incurably optimistic negro soon became attached to the country and devoted to his white folks.[14]

Katz tells us that this passage was not written by white Southerners; it appears in the 1940 printing of the widely used college text The Growth of the American Republic,[15] by Samuel Eliot Morrison and Henry Steele Commager, Professor of American Government and History at Amherst College. Katz comes to a conclusion similar to that of many other American historians mentioned later.

Although the Negro has played a significant role in history since the dawn of civilization, his contributions have been ignored by historians and his face has rarely appeared in history texts.

The distortion of the Negro's past has always had a purpose. The assertion that the Negro has no history worth mentioning is basic to the theory that he has no humanity worth defending. Deliberate misinformation has been used to justify slavery and discrimination.[16]

Besides persons who feel a need to correct a distorted verson of American history, there are also those who view black history as an "instrument of liberation" from "physical and psychological captivity." James Banks, in an article entitled "Teaching Black Studies for Social Change,"[17] insists this should be the public schools' main objective. Orlando Patterson, in a different vein, feels one must become less concerned with black history as a part of American history and perhaps focus on an entirely different content as well as technique and method. In "Rethinking Black History," Dr. Patterson argues that since the main audience of the black historian demands of him that his works serve not only intellectual but political and moral ends, a consideration of the relationship between black history and black pride by black historians is necessary.

With regard to Patterson's last point, related to black pride, Dwight Hoover, commenting on the uses of black history in his book Understanding Negro History,[18] suggests that the major problem for American historians teaching the black experience is the problem of how to explain failure. Hoover states that American history as it has been recorded is a history of success and progress. The black past, however, does not fit into this mold. To further complicate the matter, Hoover tells us that both black and white Americans proclaim the same values of liberty and equality, and their visions of the ideal society are identical. In spite of the fact that black people suffered from the total cultural impact of slavery, the conflict between black and white is still not couched in terms of two cultures, alien and American. The black experience is summarized as one in which an entire group of people has failed to be fully accepted into American life, America being a very success-oriented society; because of this powerful value orientation, one of the major problems with black history is how to fit it into a framework of progress and success. The problem of failure has been handled in different ways by different authors on the subject, who sometimes address different audiences. The views of three authors of this topic, selected by Hoover, were summarized as follows:

Samuel Dubois Cook, in an article entitled "A Tragic Conception of Negro History,"[19] argues that black history should be used to modify American history. Cook accepts as given the failure of the Negro to achieve full equality in American life; but rather than explaining it away, he sees Negro history as a corrective to American optimism.

Dwight Hoover suggests, "There is no reason why history should not be tragic; a tragic view of life may be nearer reality than any other. Nor is failure less instructive than success."[20] He also comments on William B. Hixon's article entitled "Negro Revolution and the Intellectuals."[21]

> Negro history provides an effective counterargument of the consensus view of American society as being devoid of serious conflict. For Hixon, the presence of an un-assimilated group, regardless of the moral drawn from the failure to assimilate, is of paramount importance. Negro history provides a severe critique of American society and forms the basis for a reconstruction of that society. Hixon's critique is a radical one, looking to the transformation of society. Hixon would use Negro experience to change ideas and then society.[22]

Finally, Charles Wesley, in an attempt to explain the failure of black people in America in an article entitled "Creating and Maintaining an Historical Tradition,"[23] also appearing in Hoover's book, is very much in favor of black history as a tool. Again, in Hoover's words:

> Using Jewish history as an example, Wesley claims that a knowledge of past triumphs, often achieved in the face of almost hopeless odds, will instill group pride in the present generation. Failure is caused by the strength of the opposition; even limited success shows the courage and persistence of heroic individuals.[24]

Louis R. Harlan, Professor of History, University of Maryland, expresses concern with the instrumental approach in the classroom.

> I appeal to you to give compensatory emphasis to the role that black people have played in the American past, but, on the other hand, to avoid the new distortions which would come from a propagandistic use of history to promote Negro cultural nationalism and separatism. This is not to deny that an oversimplified "cherry tree" history may serve to promote Negro pride or white compassion, but such uses of history are better left to the public outside of the classroom door.[25]

Nathan Hare, former interim chairman, Department of Black Studies, San Francisco State College, states:

> . . . Two key functions of black studies are building ego-identity and ethnic confidence for the black student. . . . The major motivation of black studies is to entice black students (conditioned to exclusion) to greater involvement in the educational process. Black studies is, above all, a pedagogical device.[26]

Edwin Fenton, Professor of History, Carnegie-Mellon University, advises school systems.

> Studying the lives of blacks in the American past may help black students to identify with their nation. . . . But improving children's self-concepts is only one appropriate objective of a full social studies program for black students. Choosing textbooks by measuring the degree to which they include biographical material about black Americans may result in the adoption of inferior social studies materials. . . . If these trends develop, the real battle for meaningful curriculum reform may well be lost.[27]

Another view which favors revision of American history but cautions against extremism in the opposite direction is posed by the Rev. Joseph Devlin, director of secondary education, New England Province, Society of Jesus:

> The rewriting of American history to give the Negro his rightful place is long overdue. But we have to watch out that we don't get into a sort of ethnic race to see who has done the most for America. This is not telling our history "like it was." It merely substitutes one unreality for another.[28]

And finally, separate courses for whites only is viewed as a realistic approach by Carl T. Rowan, former director, U.S. Information Agency:

> It's long overdue that education should provide meaningful information about the history of the Negro—but the courses should be for whites, not blacks. Any black who majors in that study ought to have his head examined.[29]

BLACK STUDIES AND THE PUBLIC SCHOOLS: WHAT IS THE STATUS?

Despite the conflicting opinions many educators have about black studies courses, the conflict over whether the nation's elementary and secondary schools should teach black studies seems to be over. The above quotes were compiled for an Education U.S.A.[30] survey of public, private, and parochial schools across the nation in 1970. This survey showed that a great number of school districts, large and small, were attempting to set up some kind of black studies program or to add material about blacks to regular history courses.

Exactly what do schools mean when they say "black studies"? is one of the questions raised in the survey. There are certainly many definitions and approaches. Other names are often used, such as cultural heritage studies, race relations minority studies, and interethnic studies. In order to communicate clearly what is going on in public schools in the area of black studies, a definition of the three main approaches used should be defined. First, cultural heritage studies are primarily the study of the black experience intended for blacks. The second approach to black studies is an integrative or thematic approach, which is the inclusion of information about the black experience, social cultural, historical, into existing courses of history, government, or social studies. Such courses include many minority groups and often include intra- and intergroup relations as well as facts about the contributions, history, and heroes of black people.

The debate then centered around whether elementary and secondary schools should offer separate courses in the various kinds of black studies or integrate this material into regular classes. The Education U.S.A. survey found that nearly all educators believed that the ultimate and ideal way to handle material on blacks and other ethnic groups was to weave it into the regular curriculum as an integral part of everything that is taught from kindergarten to grade 12.

The report stated that the integrated curriculum was already a reality in many elementary schools. For these younger children, material on ethnic groups is woven into social studies and other courses, sometimes as a separate unit but almost never as a separate course.

The approach was almost always for older students in junior and senior high schools. Many educators felt that before they could integrate the curriculum at this level, or while they were doing it, they had a responsibility to offer separate courses in ethnic studies to help older students make up for the years of neglect in this area. Consequently, a good number of schools, especially those in the larger cities, are still offering separate courses in the various aspects of black studies. Other districts with students from different ethnic groups are also beginning to devise special courses about their ethnic minorities.

Although ethnic studies courses are usually found in schools with a large number of minority students, predominantly white schools are also teaching ethnic studies. Some educators feel that ethnic studies really may be more important for the white child than the minority child, and they point with pride to the number of white students enrolled in these courses.

Most school districts had moved to set up a black studies program on the basis of a policy statement from their board of education or a directive from their superintendent of schools. Although few schools have created formal guidelines or evaluation procedures for black studies programs, nearly all have developed curriculum guides, bibliographies, or other classroom materials.

The following chapter focuses on the content of curriculum guides in black studies developed by sixteen school districts.

NOTES

1. National Advisory Committee on Civil Disorders Report, as quoted by Dr. James A. Tillman, "The Riot Commission Report:

19

1968," pp. 237-241 in Chronicles of Black Protest ed. Bradford Chambers (New York: Mentor Books, 1969), p. 238.

2. Ethnic Heritage Studies Centers, Hearings before the General Subcommittee on Education of the Committee on Education and Labor, House of Representatives, 91st Congress, Second Session, H.R. 14910, Honorable Roman C. Pucinski, Chairman (Washington, D.C.: U.S. Government Printing Office, 1970), p. 1.

3. Ibid.

4. Emergency School Aid and Quality Integrated Education Act of 1971, Report of the Committee on Labor and Public Welfare, United States Senate on S. 1557, Honorable Peter H. Dominick, Chairman (Washington, D.C.: U.S. Government Printing Office, 1971), p. 1.

5. Ibid., p. 2.

6. Ibid., p. 7.

7. Paul M. Sweezy, "Afterword: The Implications of Community Control," in Schools Against Children, ed. Annette T. Rubinstein (New York: Monthly Review Press, 1970), pp. 292-293.

8. Earl E. Thorpe, Black Historians: A Critique (New York: Morrow and Company, 1971).

9. "The Negro in American History Textbooks," casual paper of the School of Education, University of California, Berkeley, n.d.

10. Dr. Orlando Patterson, "Rethinking Black History," Harvard Educational Review 41, no. 3 (August 1971).

11. E. Franklin Frazier, Black Bourgeoisie (New York: The MacMillan Company, 1957).

12. Thorpe, op, cit., pp. 3, 4.

13. William Loren Katz, Teacher's Guide to American Negro History (Chicago: Quadrangle Books, 1958).

14. Ibid., p. 6.

15. Morrison and Commager, The Growth of the American Republic (New York; Oxford University Press, 1937).

16. Katz, op. cit., p. 5.

17. James A. Banks, "Teaching Black Studies for Social Change," Journal of Afro-American Issues 1, no. 2 (Fall 1971).

18. Dwight W. Hoover, Understanding Negro History (Chicago: Quadrangle Books, 1968).

19. Samuel Dubois Cook, "A Tragic Conception of Negro History," Journal of Negro History 45, no. 4 (October 1960).

20. Hoover, op. cit., p. 15.

21. William B. Hixon, Jr., "The Negro Revolution and the Intellectuals," American Scholar 33, no. 4 (Autumn 1964): 581-593.

22. Hoover, op. cit., p. 14.

23. Charles A. Wesley "Creating and Maintaining an Historical Tradition," Journal of Negro History 59, no. 1 (January 1964): 13-33.

24. Hoover, op. cit., pp. 14, 15.

25. National Schools Public Relations Association, Special
Report, <u>Black Studies in Schools</u> (Washington D.C., NSPRA, 1970),
p. 2.

      26. Ibid., p. 3.

      27. Ibid., p. 2.

      28. Ibid., p. 3.

      29. Ibid.

      30. Ibid., p. 2.

2

BLACK STUDIES CURRICULUM, METHODS, AND MATERIALS

In order to better understand how black studies is being approached by the school districts, a review has been undertaken, as well as a content analysis of the curriculum guides of sixteen school districts in twelve states. Each guide was prepared by a school district to assist teachers at the high school level. The guides were reviewed to determine the source of development, stated goals and objectives, topics and themes, kinds of resources suggested for use, and the kinds of related learning activities recommended.

Each guide was prepared for use in an integrated setting. The titles of the guides varied. In Alexandria, Buffalo, Chicago, Evanston, Los Angeles, and Philadelphia, the term "Afro-American studies" was used in referring to the course and its content. The term "black" was used by the districts of Cleveland and San Mateo. The more objectionable term "Negro" was used by Boston, Columbus, Dallas, Detroit, Louisville, Madison, Oakland, and Providence. Although the terms "Negro," "black," and "Afro-American" appeared to be used interchangeably in a few of the guides, it is interesting to note that each guide that used either "Afro-American" or "black" in its title had students and black teachers on the committee responsible for editing, reviewing, and/or developing the guide and its contents.

GOALS, PURPOSES, AND DEFINITIONS

In the Philadelphia guide the introduction begins with a statement that points out the objection to the term "negro" among the young:

A new mood has sprung up among Afro-Americans, particularly among the young, in which racial pride and black identity are replacing apathy and submission to the system. In fact, they no longer wish to be called "Negroes," but "black" or "Afro-American."

In all the districts visited by the author, talking with black high school students and black teachers of various political persuasions confirmed the statement in the Philadelphia guide regarding preference for terms "black" or "Afro-American." This fact poses a question regarding the lack of awareness or insensitivity on the part of administrators and other school personnel who continue to describe people using terms that the very people described consider offensive.

A number of contemporary black writers have commented on the use of the term "Negro" and what it implies. Among those who have elaborated on this derogatory classification of American blacks is Malcolm X. In Malcolm X on Afro-American History, the best arguments against the use of the term are presented in a speech given by Malcolm on Negro History Week. Among the things he criticizes regarding the teaching of black history is the use of the term "Negro."

> One of the main reasons we are called Negro is so we won't know who we really are. And when you call yourself that, you don't know who you really are. You don't know what you are, you don't know where you came from, you don't know what is yours. As long as you call yourself a Negro, nothing is yours. No languages—you can't lay claim to any language, not even English; you mess it up. You can't lay claim to any name, any type of name, that will identify you as something that you should be. You can't lay claim to any culture as long as you use the word Negro to identify yourself. It attaches you to nothing. It doesn't even identify your color.
> . . . Negro doesn't tell you anything. I mean nothing, absolutely nothing. What do you identify it with?—tell me—nothing. What do you attach it to, what do you attach to it?—nothing. It's completely in the middle of nowhere. And when you call yourself that, that's where you are— right in the middle of nowhere. It doesn't give you a language, because there is no such thing as a Negro country. It doesn't give you a culture—there is no such thing as a Negro culture, it doesn't exist. The land doesn't exist, the culture doesn't exist, the language doesn't exist, and the man doesn't exist. They take you out of existence by calling you a Negro. And you can walk around in front of them all day long and they act like they don't even see you. Because you made yourself nonexistent. It's a person who

has no history; and by having no history, he has no culture.[1]

This view of what a Negro is is not limited to black writers. Earl Conrad, a white writer who has written nine books on civil rights, has entitled his ninth book The Invention of the Negro.[2] The preface of the book describes how one night in 1964, when concern for civil rights was high throughout the nation, James Baldwin was on television talking to the white world. Angrily staring into a nation of white viewers, he said, "If I am a nigger, you invented me." His book is described as the story of that invention, which shows how, step-by-step, the "second-class" citizen was invented by the white world.

Persons involved with the development of curriculum materials and content in the area of black studies should be familiar with the concept of race, how this concept was projected throughout American history, from the drafting of the constitution through the Civil War into the civil rights movement of recent years, and how it is presently being examined by blacks in their struggle for power and identity. School districts that fail to acknowledge the factors and ideas related to institutional racism that are an operative concept in American society are not dealing with the social and political realities of American life.

This brings us to the stated goals of the various programs as outlined in the curriculum guides prepared by the school districts. The goals and purposes in the guides reviewed seemed to fall into three general categories.

1. To revise the picture of American history, which is considered biased and distorted as a result of the omission of the contributions of black people and other nonwhite minority groups.

2. To develop a sense of ethnic identity and pride among black students.

3. To improve intergroup relations by examining racism, prejudice, and other factors that have resulted in the conditions that seem to affect the progress of black people today.

Contributionism

Examples of statements under the first category, emphasizing the need to focus on the contributions of black Americans, were the following:

"In order to reflect the continuous pattern of Black life and Black contributions in the evolution of this nation, it is the conviction of the Center that the Black experience should be woven into the mainstream of American history. We believe, therefore, that Black history should be presented <u>within</u> the traditionally organized chronological United States history curriculum throughout the school year, rather than restricting it to a period of two or four weeks."—Boston

"To teach students to appreciate the contributions made by the Negro and his culture."—Buffalo

"In order to provide our students an opportunity to learn about the participation and the contributions of the black man to the American heritage . . ."—Chicago

"1. To develop an appreciation of the American Negro's African heritage and culture.
2. To examine the Negro's contributions to America.
3. To help develop the true identity of the American Negro.
4. To examine discrimination against the Negro.
5. To develop an understanding of the Negro's dissatisfaction."— Cleveland

"The primary purpose of these materials is to develop an understanding by all children that Negroes have a proud heritage and have contributed to the American way of life."—Columbus

"The primary purpose of this elective course in Afro-American History is to help students become knowledgeable about the participation and contributions of black Americans to the development of the United States and more fully aware that Afro-American history is an integral part of United States history."—Los Angeles

"This introductory unit is designed to present the Negro in his proper historical perspective: first, as a primary member of the family of mankind possessing a rich cultural heritage; and second, as the ranking minority in contemporary American society whose contributions have influenced, enriched, and broadened the American experience in spite of almost insurmountable barriers."—Louisville

"Negro history, along with the histories of varied contributions by all members of the American community, requires visibility in the story of our country—if that story is to be more than fiction."—Madison

"To understand that the Black man has contributed his unique talents to this nation in all areas of endeavor."—Providence

On the other hand there were at least two districts that renounced contributionism as an approach to black studies in favor of a black-oriented social history that would describe the new-world black experience in a hostile white environment.

> The course has been revised away from an emphasis on contributions and towards an examination of processes that have produced the unique American experience. This revision assumes that junior and senior high curricula are presently providing much of the foundation of cultural heritage that had to be initially provided by a course in Negro Culture.—Oakland

However, it should be pointed out that the Oakland guide assumes a prior knowledge of black contributions, which it feels should have been taught during the regular school program.

> Our initial premise is that the course must assist students in sorting out the complex and conflicting processes in which they find themselves participants. Events in North Oakland, Alameda County, the "third world," Chicago, their street, and all the streets of all the cities are factors in need of a system for understanding. Our objective is to use whatever confusion and conviction the students bring to the class to pursue with them questions and studies that evolve circularly, and to return with information and understandings to the original and immediate events and experiences.—Oakland

The Philadelphia guide states that "History must be corrected to relate the truth," and that "All Americans must be taught not only the truths of the present-day black man, but also the beauty and emotion of his struggle from the time of great empires through colonization, slavery, and the current reawakening." The introduction concludes:

> The history of black people in America is essentially the story of the strivings of nameless millions who have sought adjustment in a new and hostile world. The task is not to recite only his individual achievements, but rather to tell the story of the process by which the Afro-American has sought to cast his lot with an evolving American civilization. This outline is devoted to that end.—Philadelphia

In his article "Rethinking Black History,"[3] Orlando Patterson delineates and analyzes five prevailing concepts of black history; one of them is contributionism which, like the other four, he rejects for relying on fallacious assumptions concerning "civilization" and employing inadequate historical methods. He proposes various steps toward the development of an authentic black history, including less emphasis on the roles of leading blacks in a fundamentally while historical setting and a more careful study of the continuities and discontinuities between African and Afro-American culture.

There are, of course, differences of opinions among black historians and black educators as to what black history is or should be. In Black Historians: A Critique[4] Earl Thorpe divides black historians into four groups: The Beginning School, Justifiers of Emancipation, 1800-1896; The Middle Group, Builders of Black Studies, 1896-1930; The New School, Modern Scholars, 1930-1960; and the Layman as Historian. Although the author is critical of some black historians, he concludes:

> . . . All American owes the black historian great homage and respect for the splendid manner in which he has uncovered and ordered the facts of the Negro's past and published them to the eternal edification and enlightenment of all mankind. This has been a "solid service . . . rendered not merely to the Negro race, but to historical scholarship generally."[5]

In Chapter 1, "The Central Theme of Black History" he refers to black history as:

> . . . That American history which, until the 1960s, was viewed by white America with contempt and disdain or ignored altogether, just as black people themselves were viewed and treated. Men tend either to deny or force out of consciousness the evil that they do. Much of black history, then, is the story of the cruelties and inhumanities which a powerful white majority has inflicted on a defenseless black minority.[6]

Orlando Patterson elaborates on that idea by making a comparison between black history and white American history:

> Black history, as I have interpreted it, turns out to be radically different not only in content but in technique and method. White American history has been traditionally concerned with the nation state while Black history is concerned with a minority community; where the historian of white America concerns himself with

great and momentous events and the people who make them, the historian of the Black experience (and there is no reason why he may not be white) is concerned with the poor and oppressed and their quiet, unspectacular techniques of survival; where the white historian, shunning "great man" history, concerns himself with "the system," the Black historian, shunning the exceptional few who have made their contributions, concerns himself with the group; where the former develops grand theories of the rise and fall of nations, of systems of action and the like, the latter applies himself to the problem of the resilience and disintegration of preliterate cultures and the processes of acculturation. Finally, where the former seeks to illuminate his own history by comparing it with that of other nations, other systems, and other momentous events, the latter seeks to clarify his own by a comparative study primarily of other New World Blacks, but also of other oppressed peoples and oppressive conditions.[7]

Ron Edmonds, Assistant Superintendent of Public Instruction, Michigan State Department of Education, is in favor of one history called American history, which would obviate the need for a traditional American history course and a separate course in black history:

What we seek is not the addition of a number of pages or sections in texts, but an entirely new curricular and educational synthesis covering all areas of study and emphasizing (a) the experience of people whose approach to life was through their identity as members of certain groups and (b) the realities, not the dominant myths, of our history and of the social process.

Just as traditional curriculum has treated Indians as some natives encountered in the process of "building the new world," so the same curriculum has treated Blacks as a footnote to the themes of American history. The truth that must be presented is that the interaction of Black and White on this continent is a main theme of experience of the American people. No student can arrive at a realistic understanding of what has happened to the human beings who have lived and struggled under the political union of the United States without a thorough grasp of Black-White interaction; economic, social, political and psychological.[8]

Thus, it has been clearly shown that there are several possibilities for approaching the teaching and learning of black history with several very clearly defined rationales and social perspectives. Yet, except for two districts, the guides developed for the high schools invariably seem to focus on contributionism as an approach.

In some school districts black history was merely the inclusion of black personalities in a predominantly white setting. The Boston guide, for example, states:

> Knowledge about Black history should and must be accompanied by the students' understanding and awareness of the Black experience, the basic forces which have affected this nation's Black citizens.—Boston

This concern with the "basic forces" has resulted in the development of a guide for the teaching of "Negro in United States History,"as the guide is titled, no different from the American history curriculum guide. The school committee responsible for developing the guide has stated in the introduction:

> We believe, therefore, that Black history should be presented within the traditionally organized chronological United States history curriculum throughout the school year, rather than restricting it to a period of two or four weeks.—Boston

Chicago adopts a similar position with regard to their approach, as can be seen from the statement of the Superintendent of Schools in the foreword of their guide:

> The black man played an important part in American history from the very beginning. Black men came with the early explorers who opened up the New World of the Western Hemisphere. The first black Americans landed in Virginia in 1619, a year before the Mayflower landed with the Pilgrims in New England. Black men fought valiantly and died in American wars from the American Revolution to the present. They were part of the westward movement, served in the planning and building of the modern industrial and urban civilization of the nation, and contributed significantly to the development of the distinctive American culture.—Chicago

However, as can be noted by comparing the outlines of the Boston and Chicago school districts, although the approach and rationale are similar, the methods of developing the content of the course are quite distinctive. A broader perspective for the selection of topics and themes is evident in the Chicago guide. The Boston guide was developed to correlate with another United States history guide for grades 7 and 8. The Boston guide begins in the period referred to as "Discovery, Exploration and Colonization, 1492-1763." Chicago's Unit I begins with "Africa (The Beginning to 1492)." The first unit contains eighteen pages (not including three additional ones recommending instructional materials) devoted to Africa: outline of a continent, approaches to the study of history, history of the continent, and patterns of African culture before European penetration. This is the background for the next unit, "Black Men in the Americas, 1492-1787."

THE AFRICAN HERITAGE

The Chicago guide suggests a partial solution to the severe limitations of the contributionist approach to black studies curriculum. Contributionism suggests that black history unrelated to a place in traditional American history is nonexistent or at least neglible. Some guides have recognized this fallacy and include black American history as a segment of a larger historical experience. Besides Chicago, other districts that devote a chapter to the experience or heritage of Africans as background for understanding their new-world experience are the following.

School District	Chapter	Title	Total Number of Chapters in Guide
Alexandria	1	African History	8
Chicago	1	Africa (The Beginning to 1492)	5
Cleveland	1	West African Origin (one-semester course)	8
Detroit	1	Africa's Role in History	7
Los Angeles	1	The African Heritage	7
Philadelphia	1-8	Part I, Africa	16
Providence	1	African Backgrounds	8
	2	Africa's Civilization	
San Mateo	1	The African Past	6

In five other districts, Evanston, Madison, Oakland, Louisville, and Buffalo, a thematic rather than a chronological approach was used, so a chapter or section on Africa as such would not be appropriate.

However, in the Buffalo guide one of the three themes for guide twelve was "Black America in the Era of Slavery." The objective of this unit is stated as follows:

> The purpose of this first topic is to give the student an over-all view of slavery as it existed from the earliest recorded periods of man's history. From this the student will see that slavery has not been confined to the enslavement of the black man, nor was it an institution peculiar to the United States or the Western Hemisphere.
> With an understanding of slavery as it existed in the United States before the Civil War, the student will come to know the origin of the free black American who has been striving to achieve his rightful heritage and full citizenship in this country.—Buffalo

This section attempts to cover African backgrounds by outlining political, economic, and social structures of the kingdoms of Mali, Songhay, and Ghana and is prefaced, "The heritage of most black Americans can be traced to the area of West Africa touching on the Gulf of Guinea. At one time highly developed civilizations flourished in this area." However, in Columbus, Dallas, and Boston the introduction to "Negro" history, as it is called in each case, begins with the settling of America, with no reference to the background, heritage, or history of the continent from which the settlers came.

School District	Title of Chapter 1	Total Number of Chapters
Boston	Discovery, Exploration and Colonization (Beginning to 1763)	10
Columbus	Exploring and Settling in a New World	10
Dallas	The Negro During the Discovery, Exploration and Colonization of the New World (1441-1763)	13

Most of the guides that did include Africa stressed the importance of Africa as a point of departure for the study of the black experience in America.

> To understand the history of black Americans, the student must survey their origins in West Africa. While other regions contributed to the ancestral genetic pool, the majority of the black Americans' ancestors came from

the Western Sudan. From that region millions of blacks were transported under unspeakable conditions to a life of torment and toil in the New World.

Traditionally, courses in American history have largely ignored the origins of black Americans. Partly, this omission may be traced to ignorance; partly, to the mistaken belief, "Africa has no history." Such an omission has simply reinforced the prejudice of those who view the black American as a primitive without a past. Even black Americans have often been misled by this omission to the point that some have rejected any notion of links with Africa.—Cleveland

I feel it must also be pointed out that several of the school districts visited that offered courses and had developed guides in Afro-American history also had courses and guides for African history, which was treated as a separate course of study. Boston, for example, has an eighty-seven-page guide entitled "African Studies for Grades 10-12," published in 1971, since the guide on "Negro" history. The foreword of this new guide displays an awareness of the relationships between "Black Students" and their "African Heritage" and comments on the guide's being a response to the demands of black students.

. . . Africa should be studied as the place of origin of many Americans. In their quest for self-identity, self-awareness, pride and dignity, Black students are voicing demands for knowledge of their heritage. This knowledge can begin to take root in a study of the African achievement—past and present.—Boston

Black Identity

The second mentioned general category of purposes and goals for black studies was the development of ethnic identity and pride. Like Boston, many school districts confronted with demands from black students and the black community to make the curriculum more "relevant" to their needs have introduced separate courses with themes related to black identity. These districts have included in their statement of goals objectives related to improving the self-image or developing a sense of pride in African identity:

Each student should understand his purpose for being in the course and what he hopes to achieve or gain from it. This will enable him to direct himself toward

achievement of his own goals and provide self-identity—
one major objective of the course.—Alexandria

Purpose: to help destroy the myth about the
Black's cultural past in Africa—to develop an under-
standing of the cultural achievements of the early
African; to give the Black student pride in his heritage;
and to give the White student an appreciation for the
Black's cultural past.—Cleveland

Sometimes efforts by school districts to dispel myths and stereotypes about Africans and Afro-Americans, although perhaps sincere,
can be seen to be misguided. For example, the Alexandria Public
Schools, in the second unit on "African History," state their purpose
as follows:

African History first came to America via the slave
traders; but theirs was a history molded to support an
economic system. The myth they popularized showed the
Negroes as "naked savages," idle and lazy, spending their
time filing their teeth and "waiting" for the fruit to drop
into their hands.—Alexandria

A brief description of Africa follows, introducing the content to be
covered in the unit, and on the following page are concepts the teacher
is expected to develop. Some of the concepts listed are:

1. Africa cannot be described by generalizations.
   a. Africa is not a dark continent, but one which
      has a great variety of cultures, some ad-
      vanced, some not so much so.
   b. The climate of Africa is greatly varied.
   c. Africa is not a land of wild beasts.
   d. The natives of Africa are not all wild sav-
      ages.—Alexandria

Under section a, it is obvious that the term "advanced" refers to a
Western standard or criteria. Under section c, instead of stating a
negative concept to be dispelled through materials the teacher hopefully has available, it might be better to rephrase that concept to describe what it is the teacher wants to put across. Susan Hall's facts,
referred to in Chapter 3, would be a more effective way to introduce
images of Africa to dispel stereotypes. The concept outlined in section
d, "The natives of Africa are not all wild savages," many children are
already aware of, as the Harlem study cited in Chapter 3 revealed.
The world "native" has been substituted for "Africans," and implicit

in this last concept is the fact that at least some of the natives are wild savages, maybe even most. With the negative description provided in the statement of purpose, what is being accomplished is perhaps a reaffirmation of that misguided basic concept of what Africans are, along with a suggestion that perhaps in the stereotype only the percentages have been exaggerated.

Black Studies from a White Perspective

Unfortunately the effort to develop strong black self-concepts and identity fails completely when it is implemented by guides that attempt to glorify the role of blacks in the traditional white American history rather than examine black history as a discrete entity with motives, philosophies, and currents separate from and sometimes counter to the mainstream white Anglo-American or middle class history. An examination of the approaches to the study of the black experience suggested by most of the guides published by schools and districts revealed that many guides seem merely an attempt at re-editing the older version of American history that would place greater emphasis on the participation of blacks in the white American mainstream. Such approaches are being adopted by many districts that seem to have as their general goals "the integration of the black experience into the American experience."[9] As pointed out previously, this approach is not accepted by many black educators and historians as black history.

One example of this approach's failure to provide an understanding of the black experience can be seen in a book written by Mr. William Loren Katz, a teacher and textbook author whose book Teacher's Guide to American Negro History is designed to be used with curriculum guides to help teachers include the contributions of "the Negro" in United States history. Since most U.S. history courses include a unit called westward expansion, or the last western frontier, Mr. Katz suggests that included in this unit should be the exploits of the Ninth and Tenth U.S. Calvary, which composed a fifth of all the calvary assigned to pacify the West. Both these were all black regiments that patrolled from the Rio Grande to the Canadian border, from St. Louis to the Rockies. Mr. Katz also points out that it should be mentioned that "their enemies included Sitting Bull and Geronimo. . . ."[10] He further suggests that teachers should emphasize that, "Despite discrimination they [black soldiers] earned their share of Medals of Honor and could boast the lowest desertion rate in the Army."[11] It should be pointed out that this approach does not lead to an awareness of a black consciousness during that period in American history, nor does it help teachers and students understand the perceived conditions of black people during this period or their reactions to those conditions, especially, in this case, reactions of those who served in the Army. This period of history presented from a black historical perspective might better enable children to question why and whether or not black soldiers really considered Geronimo and Sitting Bull their enemies, or did the blacks and Indians become enemies as a result of the blacks' being soldiers on the side of a people whom the Indians felt were stealing their lands.

Mr. Katz also wrote another book in wide use in public schools, Eyewitness: The Negro in American History. A teacher's guide was also published to accompany that text. In Chapter 4, "Frontiersmen Conquer the Wilderness, 1800-1860," the guide lists the key concepts to be developed as well as questions for quick review. In this publication Katz provides more information related to the events of the period as viewed from different perspectives. A perceptive teacher might easily see ways in which she could help the class understand how the events of this period of American history could be interpreted differently from a black perspective than from a white one.

Key Concepts:
1. Negroes moved with each frontier wave into the wilderness,
2. Negroes and Indians often joined forces against the whites,
3. Negroes contributed toward the growth of fur trade and the exploration of Texas, Louisiana, California, and the Oregon territory,
4. Westerners opposed both slavery and free Negroes: free Negroes moving west faced insurmountable racial barriers.[12]

Questions for Quick Review:
1. As Americans moved westward, why did some slaves seek their freedom?
2. What did York contribute to the Lewis and Clark expedition? What was his reward?
3. Why were the Indians sympathetic to the Negro?
4. What proof is there that Indians did not treat Negroes as inferiors?
5. Why was the Indians' treatment of their slaves more humane than that of the white man?
6. Why did fur traders prefer Negro to white guides in the Indian territory?[13]

The intensification of racial discrimination during this period and the fact that desertion from the Army was lowest among black soldiers, as it is in today's Army, could be interpreted as a sad commentary on the social conditions in this country for black people at that time. Unless we are to assume black people are more loyal and patriotic than whites, then the Army might well have been viewed then, as it is today by many blacks, as the best of all the bad places to be in a racist society where opportunities for blacks are limited by racial discrimination and prejudice. To discuss the role of the black soldiers' enlistment in the Army during this period of American history as a contribution of the Negro is misleading if some background on the social conditions of black people during this era is not provided to enable students to see the role of black people from a broader perspective than is presented by most United States history textbooks.

Another period covered by all of the curriculum guides is the period just after the Civil War. Most materials I reviewed failed to emphasize that blacks were present all over the United States during this period. However, given the fact that their alternatives were so limited (some states even voted to expel free blacks), a result of their having been a kidnapped, exploited, and badly oppressed minority, many blacks were willing to serve as mercenaries participating in the exploitation and subjugation of another people, the American Indian, with whom they had more in common than they did with the white man in view of the fact that both groups had suffered at the hands of the same white oppressors. Whatever activities black people may have performed in the armed service of this country during that time were certainly not viewed by them as a contribution, but rather as an unfortunate consequence of existing conditions, which caused Indians and blacks to become victims of the same circumstances and played them off against each other.

However, returning to the "contribution of the Negro" as the theme for this or any other period of American history, teachers should be aware of the fact that there are concerns for students to consider. Dr. Orlando Patterson goes so far as to state that the contributionist approach to the reinterpretation of the black past is ideologically bankrupt and is methodically and theoretically deficient. No matter how arbitrary the social use of the term "black" or "Negro," one basic requirement must go with it; according to Patterson the term must be subjectively meaningful to the people so designated. For example, for Katz' description of the Negro's participation in the Army to measure up to Patterson's criteria of historical accuracy would require that the blacks in the Army considered it in their best interests as Negroes or blacks to destroy the Indian nations. However, a black point of view exercised by them as a unified people with a broader perspective might have led to their uniting with the Indians as, indeed, was sometimes the case. None of the curriculum guides reviewed in this study included or referred to views on this subject expressed during that period by outspoken blacks, such as Bishop Turner, who had served as a chaplain in the Army and was later dismissed as a result of racial discrimination.

In 1883, after the Supreme Court nullified the Civil Rights Act of 1875, Turner advocated return to Africa of blacks who could make a contribution. Turner did not view civil rights as a political issue but as one that "involves existence, respect, happiness and all that life is worth"; and having become convinced that the black man could not enjoy those rights in the United States, this ex-officer of the United States Army declared that the court decision "Absolves the Negro's allegiance to the general government [and] makes the American flag to him a rag of contempt instead of a symbol of liberty."[14] Moreover, Turner stated the Constitution itself was a "dirty rag," a cheat, a libel and ought to be spit upon by every Negro in the land. The only alternatives Turner could see were Africa or extermination.

To men like Turner, Blyden, David Walker, and many others the contributionist position might have seemed "ideologically repugnant," as it does today to many black students who have an awareness of self and who, in an attempt to develop pride in self, have rejected the need to adopt a white criterion, his "contribution" to "progress," as the standard by which to measure a black man's worth. For this reason the curriculum guides have not classified as leaders black men like Nat Turner, Gabriel Prosser, Denmark Vessey, Paps Singleton, and thousands of others who were brave and fought and died for their own and black people's freedom from white tyranny and oppression. How many schools are named after them or how many textbooks refer to them as heroes or brave men? In brief, who is going to determine which black people are worthy of mention? To a large extent this is what the argument over black studies is about.

It has been said that one of the main reasons for racism is the profit motive. For example, even the elementary school children interviewed in the Harlem survey felt Hollywood made movies stereotyping blacks unfavorably because they made money. Black playwrights, producers, directors, and actors are testing this theory. Recently a number of pictures about American history, from a black perspective, have been produced and seem to be doing well. If this trend continues, Hollywood may take the lead over the textbook publishers in reexamining history and the national myths. Excellent examples are two recent pictures, both of which take place in the West after the Civil War. The first, Soul Soldier, the story of the Ninth U.S. Calvary Regiment, was advertised this way in the New York Sunday News: "They were black troopers who fought and killed the red man for a white government that didn't give a damn about either one!"[15] The other movie, The Legend of Nigger Charley, was announced in the same paper in an ad that shows three black cowboys standing defiantly by the fence of a ranch, each armed with a determined look on his face. The caption under the almost full-page ad reads, "Somebody warn the West. Nigger Charley ain't running no more."16 The latter film was released through Paramount pictures. Perhaps persons convinced of the inherent racist nature of the American society may be in store for a surprise. It may well turn out that in terms of American values, the preservation of national myths pertaining to race may show up as a poor second, out-distanced only, however, by the profit motive.

Thematic Approach to Black Studies

The third general category of goals and purposes for black studies programs was said to be the improvement of intergroup relations by examining various factors related to the progress of black people today. Such goals seem to call for the abandonment of the traditional sequential approach to history instruction. Some districts choose to present the black experience using a theme instead of a chronological or sequential approach. These include Evanston, Madison, Cleveland, Buffalo (grade 12), and Oakland. The Madison guide is a comprehensive curriculum bulletin that suggests themes, approaches, and methods and materials for the following grades: kindergarten through grade 3, grade 5, grades 8 and 9, grade 11, and grade 12.

The high school grades 11 and 12 have two themes that the guide refers to as instructional episodes. In grade 11 the teaching episodes are comprised of a supplementary unit called the "Negro Population in America," which focuses on "the great black emigration and what it means to America." It is pointed out that this episode could fit into a contemporary history course in its relationship to the general study of population and its change. The following two objectives are listed:

1. To make predictions about the future trends in black-white relations in the North and South,
2. To identify and evaluate the relationship between demographic factors and social change.

The course also lists five understandings suggested:

1. The relationships between black and white Americans in different parts of the country have experienced change because of the alteration in the distribution of the Negro population,
2. The direction of migration within the United States has been rural to urban, south to north, and urban to suburban,

3. The black American has been the participant, as well as the victim, of the migration patterns of the United States,

4. Because of urban developments, population increases and changes in the national and racial composition of migrant labor groups, the problem of the American Negro is different than it was before World War II,

5. Those who are most likely to react with the greatest degree of dissatisfaction are those who are closest to achievement of a particular goal.

Several related learning activities are suggested, as well as a number of materials related to the goals, and the evaluation procedure is outlined in the guide as follows:

Part of the evaluation by the teacher should involve change in awareness and attitude by the student from beginning to end of the unit. Emphasis should be given to the validity of the projections rather than the assumed accuracy.

There is a quiz at the end of the unit on "Distribution of the Negro Population in America" consisting of thirteen multiple-choice questions with four response alternatives. All of the questions refer to facts that would certainly indicate whether there was an awareness of certain factors related to the demographic characteristics of the black population. The question of whether this knowledge is indicative of or leads to a change in attitude and, if so, in what direction is probably a little more than the average classroom teacher is prepared to discover by merely introducing the materials and following the procedures suggested.

In the sociology course the theme "The Black American: A Search for Identity" is presented. The function of this unit is explained as follows:

The primary function of this unit is to provide the student with opportunity to apply the concepts and understandings of Unit II (with emphasis on "Identification" and "psycho-social needs")—for the purpose of developing empathy with the search of the modern American Negro for personal identity. This difficult quest involves two distinct but closely related tasks:

1. The Negro (as well as the white community) must reject the demeaning and demoralizing mythology which has been designed to serve as his rite of passage

into the white world of upward mobility and material affluence. The relative safety of this stereotype must be relinquished before the second phase—the creation of a new and "true" image—can be begun.

2. If the rejection of the old is difficult, the assumption of the new is more so because of the necessity of bringing into accord two almost contradictory elements: the heritage of historical greatness, which the myth has forced the Negro to renounce; and the unsatisfactory contemporary conditions, which reflect the myth and misrepresent the man—to Negro and white worlds alike.

This approach is perhaps inappropriate for black students in the Madison school system. This is largely because the problem of the myth of the "Negro" is felt by many black students to be a white problem and, as James Baldwin suggests, there is very little black people can or should be expected to do that would remove the need of many insecure white people to create a "nigger." Black students ask what there is to be gained by having themselves subjected to a discussion of their personal reactions to problems with the very people who are considered by blacks to be part of the problem. An example of such a discussion topic is "Totalitarianism is an attempt on the part of a ruling elite to completely control all people within a geographic region." As a further explanation the guide goes on to state:

In this unit, slavery is viewed as a totalitarian system, in terms of cumulative effect upon the individual. The goal is to help the student develop empathy for the victim of totalitarianism, in order that he may better understand the difficulties of today's Afro-American in his search for identity against the background of slavery.

Some of the following concepts and understandings, which the guide suggests helps white children understand the problem, are presented from a white perspective—which may be appropriate for a city like Madison with only a 3 percent black population, but how do these concepts relate to the needs of black students for image and identity?

Continual frustration has a negative affect on the self-image of young people, which tends to perpetuate a cycle of poverty, despair and a general lack of identity (self-esteem).

40

The student should understand the effect of the ghetto upon its black residents.

The student should also see the relationship between civil rights activity and the development of the self-concept of the participant.

How successful have been the civil rights organizations which emphasize non-violent techniques?

What kind of changes are needed to give the Afro-American a sense of worth and dignity?

How can society best satisfy the needs of the black American without a breakdown in our social order?—Madison

One of the five student activities suggested by the guide is the following: "If there are Negro members in the class, ask them if they would like to describe how they feel about themselves as a result of their own experiences." The response of the black students to the Madison school system in general and to its approach to black studies in particular is covered in the case studies in Chapter 3, which were obtained by the author during his visit to the Madison school district.

Criticism being raised is directed toward the methods and approach of the Madison school district rather than the objectives or goals of the guide, which are quite the same as those of many other school districts. An example of a more desirable and effective approach to understanding the black experience from a black's point of view would be that developed by Evanston Township High School in Illinois. This school has developed a course in Afro-American Creative Expression to help achieve goals and objectives similar to those of the Madison high schools. The course, which was developed through the Speech and Arts Department, is divided into three sections: "The Arts and the Senses," "The Tribe Free and the Tribe Restricted," and "The Black Artist—What He Is Saying."

The objectives of the guide are evaluation techniques stated as follows:

The format of the Guide is arranged so that each left-hand page contains suggested activities which are directed to the student, while the right-hand page is directed to the teacher in terms of procedures and instructional emphases.

The Behavioral Evidences of Student Awareness and Response are suggested lists of observable behaviors which may be used to evaluate student achievement. In most cases, space has been provided for the teacher to add additional evidences as he observes them during the year.

The Guide is intended to be flexible in its approach. The teacher may use only those suggested activities which he thinks necessary to fulfill the stated objectives, and he is encouraged to add his own so long as he fulfills the student objectives of the section he is teaching.—Evanston

In section III, "The Black Artist—What He Is Saying," the following suggested teacher emphases for learning activities are listed:

1. To begin to discover some basic elements of black life-style,
2. To make the student more aware of the uniqueness of the black experience and to discover whether or not that experience can be recreated by an author who is not black.

The activities in this unit provide opportunities for black students to do the following:

5. to demonstrate the ability to create improvisations which mirror his black experience,
6. to use the theatre experience as a means of achieving awareness of self and belief in self,
7. to discover the theatre as a means of communicating the ethnic life of the black culture,
8. to discover if and how the contemporary black playwright mirrors the black experience,
9. to recognize the theatre as one means of developing social change and for mirroring social conflict,
10. to discover the theatre as a "means of survival",
11. to begin the search for a black life-style in the theatre; and, if none is discovered, to begin to create one.

The emphases of the various learning experiences for all children are to develop "self-awareness" and "self-concept." Some of the methods of evaluation are listed as follows:

BEHAVIORAL EVIDENCES OF STUDENT AWARENESS AND RESPONSE:
If the objectives of this section are realized, each student will demonstrate, to a degree, behavioral evidences similar to the following:

(Activity 1) Will demonstrate, as a participator,
his empathy with a situation that is uniquely black.

May make such statements as "We never do that in
our church," or "If you believe, you gotta get involved,
really involved", or "That's one trait that's black."

(Activity 2) Will demonstrate, through discussion,
his ability to recognize differences between black and
white playwrights in their approach to the black experience.

May make such statements as "He's got the idea,
but he doesn't SAY it right."

(Activity 8) Will demonstrate more awareness of
the black experience and its uniqueness and will search
for and evaluate its blackness. "That's black!! That
could only be black!!!"

Similar to the Madison schools, the Evanston Township High
School student population is predominantly white, but integrated. The
needs of the black and white students in both districts could be described as being the same. The course in Evanston is designed to
meet the needs of black students and, in the author's opinion, the
Evanston course is felt to be a more valid and effective approach to
an understanding of the black experience than is the Madison one. In
Evanston while the black student is expected to become personally
involved in an attempt to understand how the black experience is
portrayed in theatre, music, art, and other cultural forms, he is not
on the spot as an informant trying to explain to others what it feels
like to be black when he has not learned how to approach that question
in an emotionally constructive, analytical, and subjectively meaningful
context.

A RELEVANT BLACK CURRICULUM AND ADAPTATION
OF CURRICULUM GUIDES TO LOCAL NEEDS

In most of the high schools visited by the author, guides developed by the school districts for teaching black studies were not in
use. Many teachers complained that the guides were not very helpful
in dealing with certain types of learner attitudes nor did they stress
or emphasize what the black students or black community defined as
black studies. In his Black Curriculum: Developing a Program in
Afro-American Studies,17 Sidney Walton spells out what he refers to
as creative black solutions for teachers who desire specific "how to
do it" pointers and methodology. The needs of black students, as
defined by those students and their communities and summarized in

43

this book, point out major discrepancies between the programs school districts are developing and those being advocated and demanded by the communities and black students. For example, the following themes are very much related to the needs and interests of black students living in ghettos and could be handled in the regular school program through either existing or newly developed courses:

Social and Economic Conditions in Ghettos
Civil Rights Laws, 1965 to Present
Community Responsibility in Government
Consumer Education
Origin and Migrations of Ethnic Groups
Racism

The following themes or topics were the only ones covered by the sixteen guides reviewed related to the above categories:

Buffalo
    Black Protest Thought
    The Black Man in Contemporary Society
Madison
    The Black American: A Search for Identity
Cleveland
    The Quest for Black Identity: What's in a Name?
      Black, Negro, Colored or Afro-American?
    The Ghetto: Black Prison or Black Community?
    The Black Entrepreneur in a White Economy: Competitor or Survivor?
    Black Education: Black Needs or White Standards?
    The Black Church: Venerable Institution or Dynamic Force?
    The Black Artist: Chiefly Black or Chiefly Artist?
    The Black Protest Movement: Integration or Separatism?
    Black Power: Old or New?
Oakland
    Black Consciousness, Genius, Ethical Lessons for America
    Reassessment of Contemporary Phenomena
Chicago
    The Struggle for Civil and Human Rights, 1914 to Present
Los Angeles
    The Black American's Search for Civil Rights Since World War II
Detroit
    The Search for Equality, 1945 to Present
Columbus
    The Civil Rights Movement

Dallas
America's Civil Rights Movement
Alexandria
Afro-American Activism: America's Civil Rights Revolution
Philadelphia
The Search for an Identity: Racial Self-Expression
Black Nationalism and Black Power
Epilogue: The Destruction of Cultural Memory
Louisville
Social, Economic and Political Problems
Tools for Possible Solution of Social, Economic and Political
   Problems
The Search for Leadership

As can be seen from the offered topics, few of the courses are related
to contemporary social and economic conditions in ghettos, community
responsibility in government, consumer education, racism, or origin
and migrations of ethnic groups. Of all of the topics previously suggested as related to the needs and interests of black students living in
ghettos, civil rights is the only area in which progress seems to have
taken place and which is included as a topic in most of the course lists.
    Following is the index of civil rights achievement or progress
used by several of the school districts.

Even after decisions by the Supreme Court, the drama-
tic march on Washington in 1963, and the untiring efforts
of organizations and individuals—Negro and white—the
Negro still finds it necessary to protest.—Louisville

1. The United States Supreme Court has played a
substantial role in bringing about civil rights reform.
    2. The United States Supreme Court decision in
1954 entitled Brown v. The Board of Education was a
significant milestone in the breakdown of segregation
in the United States.
    3. Although major gains have been made by the
Negro, prejudice and inequality still remain in the
United States.
    4. The 1954 decision did not bring an end to segre-
gation.
    6. The civil rights cause is divided today.
    9. Non-Violent tactics take more "guts" than
violent methods of protest.
    11. The Negro has a long way to go to achieve
total equality.

12. There is a great deal of racism in America today.—Alexandria

In spite of many obstacles, the Afro-American has progressed toward equality since the Emancipation Proclamation. Negroes have taken advantage of their opportunities, but their opportunities have been too few. The civil rights movement has not brought total equality of opportunity for Negroes, but it has made progress in this direction.—Columbus

3. Concepts for the 1960s
   a. The spread in Civil Rights activities to the North made many non-black people realize that the problem was not sectional, but nationwide.
      (1) Riots in the northern cities had great effects on the nation
      (2) "White backlash" and black violence became threats to the Civil Rights movement
   b. In spite of legal gains black people were not satisfied with the progress made between 1945 and 1968.—Detroit

A. Opportunities remain limited for black youth to enter into the mainstream of American life.
B. Some black people now reject any opportunity to become part of the established system, preferring to rely upon their own black institutions and black leaders.
C. The deplorable urban riots throughout the nation reflect the degree to which anger, frustration, and hostility have contributed to the alienation of some black people.
D. Current governmental responses to the needs for advancement of the black American are beginning to produce far-reaching legislation.
E. The efforts of many, black and white, are beginning to evidence a change toward a better way of life for the black American and thus for the betterment of the nation in general.—Los Angeles

The march in Washington, D.C., in August of 1963, served notice that America's Negroes were no longer willing to wait generation after generation for rights that other Americans take for granted.

The march from Selma, Alabama, to Montgomery,
Alabama, led to the passage of the 1966 Voting
Rights Bill.—Chicago

Some districts that have developed guides seem to encourage the
local schools and teachers to determine which topics or themes are
most appropriate for the schools in their particular district. In Los
Angeles, for example, one of the main purposes of the guide, as described by the Division of Instructional Planning Services, which was
responsible for its development, is to provide direction, stating further
that the adaptation to local needs was the professional responsibility
of the teacher in each class. The cooperation of teachers in the Los
Angeles district was requested in recommending alterations and
evaluating the usefulness of the guide as a teaching aid. Teachers
were assured that their feedback would serve as the basis for a more
complete publication, which the district was planning to publish and
which would include sample learning activities, evaluation devices,
and bibliographic references for teachers.

In Chicago the school boards consulted well-known black historians to advise a committee composed of teachers and staff of the
Board of Education and have copyrighted their guide. In notes to the
teacher it is explained that the curriculum guide has been prepared
to help all teachers who are attempting to bring insight into the role
and contributions of Afro-Americans in relation to the history and
culture of our nation.

In Detroit a workshop of teachers was held by the Department of
Social Studies to prepare a guide. Each participant prepared specific
units of study for the course. The guide suggests effective ways to
use a specific textbook and further states, "The course will be much
more meaningful and motivating to the pupils if the suggested variety
of materials and methods is used to develop the informational background." The guide is copyrighted, with all rights reserved.

In Columbus, Ohio, the steering committee that assisted in the
development of their guide expressed the opinion that although materials on Negro history and culture are being published in increasing
quantity, "An interim publication such as this would be useful in providing teachers with background information that could be used until
such a time as more suitable published materials become available."

New York State developed a manual entitled "Afro-American
Studies," the outline of which was adopted by the Buffalo Public Schools.
In the New York state manual a similar concern is expressed concerning the abundance of materials: "This manual is designed to help the
non-specialist cope with the existing body of material on Afro-American
studies and establish guidelines for evaluating new resources as they
appear."

Some of the districts expressed optimism and confidence that their guides would lead to improved instruction:

This teacher's resource is a milestone in curriculum development in Philadelphia. It is the result of the combined efforts of community participants, students, university specialists and the school district personnel. Teachers will find it a most useful source of background material not readily available in many school texts.— Philadelphia

This guide is intended to help develop creative methods of teaching the history of Black Americans. It is fresh, even novel in approach. It should stimulate imaginative instructors to teach effectively this important phase of American history.—Cleveland

This Curriculum Guide represents a continuation of the progress made by the Buffalo Public Schools in providing students and teachers with an up-to-date and accurate presentation of the role of the black man in the development of American life.—Buffalo

This curriculum guide is another step forward in the constant effort to meet the needs of our pupils, our teachers and the changing times. Its preparation involved the talents and high professional competence of many experienced teachers, as well as supervisory and administrative personnel.—Boston

However, the Boston School District was careful to add, "The effectiveness of this curriculum guide, as that of any other tool, will depend upon the skill of the user."

On the other hand, a few districts expressed reservations regarding the usefulness of their guides:

This booklet was written as a tentative guide for the teaching of Afro-American Studies in Alexandria. The booklet certainly has many shortcomings which will need correction, as only a portion of the materials was tested on the students during the summer of 1969.— Alexandria

More Effective Ways of Organizing Instruction
and Selecting Teaching Materials

Concepts of Black History

Earl Thorpe in Black Historians states that most of American
history (white) has had as its theme national progress. According to
Thorpe, American history has played up the achievements of a people
living under the conditions of "freedom and democracy." He refers
to statements made by Henry Steele Commager in his book The American Mind.

> A people so aware that they were making history were
> conscious of their duty to record it. A people sure that
> they were beating out paths for other nations to follow
> were sensible of the obligation to make those paths well.
> A people whose institutions were continually under scru-
> tiny were zealous to explain and defend them. A people
> so proud of their achievements and so uncontaminated by
> modesty were eager to celebrate their triumphs. A people
> made up of such conglomerate elements and with so little
> racial or religious or even geographical unity were at
> pains to emphasize their common historical experience
> and validate their historical unity. A people whose col-
> lective memory was so short were inclined to cherish
> what they remembered and romanticize it.[18]

Dr. Thorpe points out that only a casual acquaintance with black historical literature would reveal that many of the above generalizations
do not apply, and black historians aware of these forces and impressions
have not been accepted as respected members of the American community. When pointing out the magnificent achievements of Americans
"under democracy and freedom," the black historian presents this as
the background to show how the treatment of his race has been a violation of this record. Yet in spite of the influence of the many new
historical theories and movements, the black historians have denied
there is anything unique or peculiar about the black man insisting he
is "just like any other average human being." Such is the pattern
woven throughout the fabric of black history as presented by black
historians.

Since the colleges that train history teachers have not seen fit
to modify the existing version of American history or develop new
courses in black history, answers to the question "how to make black
history relevant in the public schools?" have fallen into the hands of
the educators by default. There is general agreement among the

49

historians and those in teacher education that some sort of black history is necessary, even if only a reinterpretation of white history. The questions of topics, themes, objectives, learning activities, and materials are promised solutions by educators occasionally using the historians as consultants to guarantee accuracy rather than define content.

Furthermore, there are various philosophies related to the teaching of black history. Often the philosophy is an expression of the needs of the population. In Suggestions for the Teaching of Negro History Genevieve Taylor, in an article entitled "The Teaching of Negro History in Secondary Schools," mentions the needs of black youth as the rationale for development of content:

> The Negro youth when he reaches the secondary school has very often been forced to meet situations which very definitely indicate to him that he must exist in a restricted area of a complex environment. He realizes that his opportunities for employment, recreation, and sharing in the general cultural life of his community are very limited. The teacher must recognize the reality of such a problem, and help pupils understand these issues by making a historical study of their origin and development. Such materials must come within the scope of the Negro History Course.[19]

The aims for a course to meet these needs are suggested as follows:

> . . . To get an understanding of the remote and immediate background of the Negro; to correct mistaken ideas concerning his character; to help develop a sane philosophy of life; to develop self-confidence, pride in the race, openmindedness, and a common sense attitude in facing realities.[20]

Two diametrically opposed approaches to black history courses have emerged in response to these needs. On the one hand, the purpose of the pamphlet published by the Association for the Study of Negro Life and History is to help persons desiring to use the contributionist approach develop lesson plans and topics that emphasize the role of black people in the American Heroic Experience. This is referred to by each of the contributors as a means of providing black children with dignity. In one lesson plan entitled "A Lesson Plan for Teaching Negro History in the Fifth Grade," Edyth H. Ingraham lists the specific objectives as follows:

A. To help children recognize the relationship between the American Negro and the other American citizens,

B. To help children understand how the American Negro adjusted to the environment and made use of the resources available to him in order to gain a good life,

C. To help children to appreciate the part the American Negro has played in the cultural heritage of the United States,—To bring about desirable attitudes and behavior patterns as a result of information learned,

D. To help Negro boys and girls gain inspiration and pride in themselves and in their cultural heritage.

Her activities for accomplishing this aim were as follows:

A. Checked books and materials in class and school libraries for information.

B. Visited Children's Department of Logan Library and Fellowship Commission Library to secure books on topic.

C. Invited the President of Local Branch of Association for Study of Negro Life and History.

D. Visited Fellowship House—learned stories from Doll Library.

E. Collected pictures and articles from magazines and newspapers.

F. Compiled scrap books.

G. Wrote and made individual reports to class.

H. Made population maps and graphs showing where Negro population is the greatest; the movement to all parts of the United States; comparing Negro population with that of other Americans in our large cities.

I. Worked together in committees organizing group reports and constructing an exhibit of stand-up-cut-out pictures. Saw and discussed films. Read and enjoyed the True Comic Book "Negro Heroes."

J. Wrote and presented an original Radio Quiz Program for Assembly.

K. Prepared an original pageant for "I AM AN AMERICAN DAY."[21]

Compare the above goals and approaches with that of the National Association of Afro-American Educators in their NAAAE Anniversary Edition of the Black Curriculum, also published in 1969. One of the purposes of this edition, Developing a Program in Afro-American Studies, is stated by Preston Wilcox in the foreword:

> This book is the first major work by a Black author which masterfully emphasizes and utilizes the concept of ACCOUNTABILITY for the learning and educating of Black youngsters. Black educators throughout the nation now have a model for making teachers and administrators accountable for specific educational phases previously buried under numerous layers of "professionalism," "ethics," and other educational rhetoric.
>
> Although the author pulls no punches and truly "tells it the way it is" from a Black man's perspective, the point should be made that the integrity of a person is not challenged but rather the "functional racism" of that person is being exposed from a Black perspective. A white person is never a functional racist from his own perspective because he doesn't operate against himself as he does against the Black man.
>
> White racism is the core of our problem and until we address ourselves to that issue, we are headed for war in America.[22]

In Chapter III, "Guidelines for Establishing a Black Curriculum in a School," three of the eleven guidelines suggest an entirely different emphasis and approach for the development of a program in black studies from that of the Association for the Study of Negro Life and History. The NAAAE encourages black educators to do the following:

> B. Establish "Substance" Committee to develop the essence of the program which will be sent to the school-wide implementation committee: The Substance Committee consists of:
> Black Student Union representatives
> "Negro" student representatives
> All biologically Black faculty members
> Paid outside Black professional consultants
> Representatives from the Black community
> E. Set Definite Black Determined Deadlines for Implementation
> Comment:
> Most Black people must change their expectations of the present system before they seek an education in that system.

52

What we have to do is to equip ourselves to change the system so that we can get an education, BEFORE we go into that system. Anything else is pure folly.

    F. Goals and Objectives
        Student Involvement
        Teacher Involvement
        Community Control[23]

Critics of both the ASNLH and the NAAAE approach have stated that these two approaches incorporate the same fallacy as the school districts that publish one general teaching guide in black studies to cover the wide range of beliefs, attitudes, interests, and other differences that exist among the school population within their respective districts.

The suggestions are often either too vague and general or, on the other hand, too specific to have any practical application for persons who are not in the categories the instructional material and learning activities were designed for. The ASNLH materials advocate a "common sense" attitude to help black children face realities. It assumes that an understanding of the background of the existing social and economic realities should be provided through the schools that will help black children realize a sense of self-worth and dignity through the realization of the tremendous odds that are continually being confronted and overcome by black people. The NAAAE suggests the institution of education in the United States works to the detriment of black people and should be restructured to work in their interests. Dr. Wolfe raises two questions: (1) What do we mean by "Black Studies"? and (2) What should we teach? In answer to the first question she quotes from Lebert Bethune:

> In clarifying the meaning of "Afro-American Studies" Bethune first defines Afro-American to mean "the people of African ancestry living in the United States. It also means people of African ancestry living within the continental complex that includes North, South, Central America, and the Caribbean." He further indicates that, in spite of certain diversities of language and cultural traits, they (the Afro-Americans thus defined) share a common historical experience in the New World and a set of common cultural antecedents—African in origin. Fundamentally, they have shared a common concrete aspiration for that full freedom which they have not been heir to as long as they've been in the New World.
>   It may be useful to metaphorically represent the Afro-American experience by picturing a set of three

continuous rings, with Africa as the outermost ring, the New World as the second, and the United States as the innermost. We must consider these as related, in the sense of a dynamic and continuous unit spiralling inward and outward backward and forward. And it is the history of that spiral metaphor, the dynamics of its movement, the nature of its composition and the consideration of its contemporary attributes and problems which constitute the Afro-American experience and must, therefore, be reflected in Afro-American Studies.[24]

Dr. Wolfe summarizes:

In summary, "Black Studies" is the organizing of knowledge around the experiences of people of Africa and African descent. It is both historical and contemporary since it must deal with the experience itself with its real issues and problems as lived in the past and present. It utilizes the content, methodology, and skills of the separate disciplines of history, sociology, anthropology, psychology, literature, language, linguistics, political science, biology, geography, social welfare, economics, law, theology, music, art, and drama but is also interdisciplinary since the Black Experience is interdisciplinary.[25]

Finally, an alternative to the ASNLH and NAAAE proposals and the district curriculum guides, which have proved too general to be of use to teachers with specific needs, has been recommended by Dr. Wolfe and shows great promise toward constructively involving the community in defining its own values and goals as they relate to black studies within the context of the total school curriculum. Dr. Wolfe's approach is an attempt to get children in different places to examine their particular situations and develop understandings and solution strategies relevant to the conditions, resources, and level of need in their respective communities. One of the five purposes she lists for black studies programs is "To study the problems which Afro-Americans face in American communities today and, wherever possible, actively cooperate with individuals and organizations of the black community in their solution."[26]

A model for an effective way of accomplishing this suggestion is provided by Region One of the Detroit public school system. This predominantly black region is one of eight in the Detroit school district. The need for integrating black studies into the regular school curriculum in all areas and at all levels was given priority to the extent that the superintendent of this region appointed a full-time staff member who was given the title and responsibility of Black Studies Coordinator. In February 1972 a workshop was conducted called the Black Studies Curriculum Development Workshop. The philosophy underlying the need for a workshop was spelled out in a publication, Summary of Expressed Ideas and Aims Regarding the Development of a Black Studies Program in Region One.[27]

The problems in contemporary education that black studies would address were summarized as follows:
1. Students will be exposed to a singular culture—White.
2. Students will come to view White people as superior to Black people.
3. Students will have little opportunity to reflect and relate to other cultures.
4. Non-White students will find it difficult to form healthy and positive images about themselves.
Consequently, such an approach encourages many to see America's experiences as being only the sum total of the White man's experiences. Such insights are erroneous, misleading, and all too ethnically degrading.
A constant reinforcement of White values on Black children affords them little opportunity to build positive personal concepts about themselves, their families, or their communities. Such a denial merely leads students to an open rejection of "self," therefore, it seems reasonably appropriate to consider the matter of self-concept development as the first and probably the most important step to take in the development of a Black Studies curriculum.[28]

The purpose of black studies was then defined:

In order to build healthy self-images, the Region One Black Studies Program should enable students to:
1. come to know the importance of self-awareness;
2. know the historical and cultural events that link them to a past, present, and future;
3. value the worth of humanism as opposed to the values of materialism;
4. recognize the functional reality of Black institutions;
5. identify the nature and roles of each member of the Black family—nuclear and extended families;

6. examine and critique the behavior of self and others;

7. understand the real need for group identification.

Self-knowledge, self-awareness, and the security of group identity are sources of strength for any group. When given the tools and opportunity to attain a sense of "self," Black students should become more cognizant of their roles in society, more aware of the need for scholastic achievement, more interested in developing a constructive society, and most of all, more capable of participating effectively in a Democratic society.[29]

The attainment of a positive self-concept alone was not felt to be enough. Objectives to enable students to critique and examine events that shaped their past and present and to bring about change in their community were also listed:

In order for students to implement change in the community, the Region One Black Studies Program should:

1. Teach students to develop critical thinking skills.

2. Teach students to hold in high regard accountability to the Black community.

3. Focus student awareness on community needs and interests.

4. Direct students to a close examination of all of the possible means of bringing about political, social, and economic changes in the Black community.

5. Present to the student the opportunity to place into operation the ideas and "constructs" that they recognize as being needed in the Black community.

Finally, a need was recognized for in-service teacher education programs, evaluation of programs, and cooperation and involvement of the community:

Like any other viable part of the schools' curriculum, Black Studies can "only sustain" a continued existence when it is recognized as being a legitimate and relevant discipline. Only a well-thought-out program by parents, students, teachers, board members, and administrators will sustain such a program.[30]

Each school in the district was asked to select a black studies coordinator to work with the district coordinator. The principal of each school was invited to define the roles of the respective building coordinators. A compilation of the common skills and characteristics the coordinators felt they needed to understand and perform the tasks they outlined for themselves were prepared in the form of a report. The needs were listed under attitudes and skills:

Attitudes
     1. Committed to the Black Studies program. Willingness to give of his time and energy.
     2. Be committed to a program that will develop productive, fully functioning people.
     3. Openmindedness—receptive to other ideas and beliefs.
     4. A total-curriculum-minded person who recognizes the value of integrating Black Studies within the total curriculum.
     5. Recognizing that Black Studies is more than black history.
     6. Have a practical and realistic outlook about Black Studies as it relates to American society.
     7. Have a "together" self-image in order to build a better image within the child.
     8. Positive (non-destructive) image of the black child and his community.
     9. Appreciation of the varying backgrounds of children.
     10. An accepting attitude toward student participation.

Skills
     1. The ability to help reluctant staff members to develop a positive acceptance of the program.
     2. Knowledge and expertise in "playing the game" (economic emphasis).
     3. Knowledge of available material.
     4. Ability to evaluate and recommend appropriate age- or grade-level use.
     5. Ability to help children develop a positive self-image.
     6. Possess the skills to work effectively with others.
     7. Innovativeness—being able to help others to adapt materials to different situations.
     8. Ability to listen for the needs of students.
     9. Ability to help others to formulate likes and dislikes based upon situations and experiences, and not bias thoughts.

10. Establish "esprit de corps" among entire staff.

The common points of agreement on the roles were the following:

1. Distribute copies of lesson plans.
2. Make available sources of free and inexpensive materials.
3. Coordinate activities in building.
4. Schedule various programs.
5. Form a parity committee to deal with Black Studies in the school community.
6. Work with the parity committee to measure the effectiveness of the program.
7. Motivate staff through demonstration of all new and available material.
8. Assemble and be responsible for all materials related to black studies in your building. (Establish Resource Center.)
9. Know the total scope of the Black Studies program as it evolves in your school.
10. Act as liaison between school and Region One.
11. Be a motivating agent—one who is as enthused as he would want other staff members to be.

The following recommendations were sent to each local school administrator:

1. Willingness to permit Resource Person and/or Demonstration Teacher to help within the school day.
2. Adaptation to new ways and trends in teaching.
3. Release of necessary supplies for implementation of programs.
4. Someone in authority to work with, such as a department head, curriculum leader, etc., and a Black Studies committee.
5. All teachers must be directly involved with Black Studies at all levels, K-12.
6. All teachers who are directly involved at the planning level within school must have specified time for articulation meetings.
7. Articulation between feeder schools so that a continuity of subject matter may be possible.
8. Scheduled coordinating time for building coordinators.

9. Let the administrators assume the responsibility to see that an on-going effective Black Studies program evolves within the building.

10. That the Administrator visit all classrooms with regularity and bring pressure on those who aren't following through with the Black Studies program as instituted.

The workshop that was then held was comprised of five teams of five persons each, a principal or assistant principal from each school, a teacher, a student, a parent, and a para-professional. Each group discussed philosophy, goals, and objectives. The specific questions posed in the pre-planning sessions were:

V. STRATEGIES AND PLAN OF ATTACK
   Bettye McIntosh, Director
   A. Directional Questions
      WHY   - 1. What should a black studies program do for the students in the final analysis?
      WHAT   - 2. What should be included in a black studies curriculum?
      HOW & - 3. How should black studies be included
      WHEN   in the curriculum?
   B. Operational Questions
      1. What are some of the constraints that would prevent us from implementing an effective black studies program in the schools?
      2. How can we best utilize the first workshop?
      a. Who should participate?
      b. What should we attempt to accomplish?
      c. When should we meet?
      d. What resources should be utilized?
      3. How can we research what has been done in the area of black studies?

Out of the workshop came a twenty-eight-page report summarizing the reports of each of the five panels with specific recommendations for each of the following goals:

Goals	Number of Specific Recommendations
Community Awareness	15
Development of a "Self-Help" Program within the Black Community	10

Goals	Number of Specific Recommendations
Language—Social Development and Political Awareness	27
Political Education	16
Music	12
Literature	9
Creative Writing	15
Library	9
Economic Education	14
Art	19
Critical Examination of Mass Media	16
Science	9
Think Tank (the development of a "scientific method of problem-solving" as it relates to critical crucial issues)	10

The report is a truly representative document of a common concern about problems out of which evolved a common approach. It is the feeling of the author that process, which is a vital and critical issue in education, is as important as product. If the outcome of Detroit's community school workshop has been a document similar to the ASNLH's suggestions for teaching about Negro history, or had it produced a document closer to the NAAAE Black Curriculum handbook, the process through which the document has been produced would guarantee a greater degree of cooperation and effectiveness in reaching those desired goals than if the district had adopted a document, no matter how excellent, and then tried to achieve agreement among teachers, students, parents, and community in implementing something produced for them. To a large extent this is the author's criticism of the usefulness of the guides that were developed by school districts for teachers and students rather than with teachers and students.

NOTES

1. George Breitman, ed., Malcolm X on Afro-American History (New York: Pathfinder Press, 1970), pp. 15-16.
2. Earl Conrad, The Invention of the Negro (New York: Paul S. Erikson, 1966).
3. Patterson, "Rethinking Black History," Harvard Educational Review 41, no. 3 (August 1971).
4. Earl E. Thorpe, Black Historians: A Critique (New York: Morrow & Company, 1971).

5. Ibid.

6. Ibid., pp. 3-4

7. Patterson, op. cit.

8. 1970-71 Michigan Project, "Improving State Leadership in Education," Cultural Democracy, a Report of the Members of the Project, July 8, 1970, p. 2.

9. William Loren Katz, Teacher's Guide to American Negro History (Chicago: Quadrangle Books, 1968).

10. Ibid., p. 6.

11. Ibid., p. 7.

12. William Loren Katz, Eyewitness: The Negro in American History, Teacher's Guide (New York: Pitman, 1968), p. 24.

13. Ibid., pp. 24-25.

14. Edwin S. Redkey, "Bishop Turner's African Dream," The Journal of American History 54, no. 2 (September 1967): 271-83.

15. Advertisement, New York Sunday News, May 14, 1972, p. LS10.

16. Ibid.

17. Sidney F. Walton, The Black Curriculum: Developing a Program in Afro-American Studies (Palo Alto: Black Liberation Publishers, 1969).

18. Thorpe, Black Historians, op. cit., p. 192.

19. Genevieve Taylor, "The Teaching of Negro History in Secondary Schools," in Suggestions for the Teaching of Negro History, a publication of the Association for the Study of Negro Life and History (Washington, D. C.: Associated Publishers), p. 8.

20. Ibid.

21. Ibid., p. 12.

22. Walton, The Black Curriculum, op. cit., pp. v, vi.

23. Ibid., pp. 98-99.

24. Deborah P. Wolfe, "Integrating Black Studies into the Curriculum of Today's Schools," in Multimedia Materials for Afro-American Studies: A Curriculum Orientation and Annotated Bibliography of Resources, ed. Harry Allen Johnson (New York: R. R. Bowker, 1971), p. 60.

25. Ibid.

26. Ibid., p. 61.

27. A Report Prepared by the School Black Studies Curriculum Development Workshop, Region One, Detroit Public School System.

28. Ibid.

29. Ibid.

30. Ibid.

CHAPTER
3

IMAGES OF AFRICA

ETHNIC STUDIES AND CHANGING IMAGES OF AFRICA

During the Spring and Fall of 1970, the Bureau of Curriculum Development of the Board of Education of the City of New York conducted a survey entitled Ethnic Studies in the New York City Public Schools. In stating the rationale for the survey, the Bureau concluded:

> It can be posited that focusing upon the strengths of a subculture can reduce much of the tension, anxiety, and self-hatred deriving from ethnic neglect and mistreatment, thereby permitting of a more positive and controlling response to the environment. The image of self and of race will be enhanced and reinforced as the feeling of worth and dignity grow. A more confident and affirmative attitude toward self and society, it is reasonable to assume, will motivate pupils to greater effort and interest in school work.[1]

Although no effort to substantiate the above proposition was made by the Bureau, which conducted the survey among 856 of the city's 922 public schools, it was established that a major proportion of the city schools have introduced ethnic or cultural heritage programs. The study revealed that 617 of the 856 schools that reported had ongoing programs dealing with ethno-cultural studies. This represented 72.1 percent of the city schools sampled on all levels. Manhattan, Bronx, and Brooklyn have the majority of their students in minority group categories, as reported in the Annual Census of School Population, October 31, 1969, published by the Bureau of Educational Research and Statistics. Yet even the two boroughs with a majority of white pupils, Queens and Richmond, had introduced these courses. On a city-wide basis, black studies was cited most often by the schools responding as the subject of most of these courses. Since black pupils comprise the largest minority group in the city, this might be expected.

The trend suggested by the survey was that a greater felt need was leading to an increase in such courses and programs, and the study reported that several provocative problems were posed by the data. One of the problems posed was the following:

> With evidence of the widespread introduction of ethno-cultural programs involving many students, it becomes incumbent upon educators to assess the impact of this endeavor. By means of experimental research studies and evaluation procedures applied to ongoing programs, the differential effects of various aspects of these studies can be elucidated. For instance, it would be of interest to know whether, in fact, there is a dynamic reference of this material to the self and what form it takes. Furthermore, its role in the development of attitudes towards others, and the behaviors derived from those attitudes may also come to light. It would be of consequence to know whether any positive gains from these studies enhance motivation toward academic achievement generally and improve learning in other subjects.[2]

The Board of Education's Research Report suggested an area of research in relation to the above questions:

> Although it is as yet too new to be tested for verification of its impact upon pupils, there is, nevertheless, strong presumptive validity that the introduction of ethno-cultural studies into the classroom will provide a sustaining impetus to improved learning by minority children. The values anticipated are of three types—psychological, social, and educational.[3]

By coincidence, this premise was being examined by the author in the Spring of 1969 when, as Director of In-Service Teacher Education Programs at the African-American Institute at United Nations Plaza in New York, he conducted a survey among three elementary schools in New York City's School District #6 in Manhattan. Each school had organized separate classes in African studies for the first time. The schools were P.S. 175, P.S. 197, and P.S. 192. The schools had assigned special teachers who taught only African studies to students in the fourth, fifth, and sixth grades. African study sessions were held once or twice a week for an hour, allowing each teacher to

handle between twelve and fifteen classes a week. This was called a
cluster program. The courses were described as African heritage
courses, whose major goals were to help children "develop respect
and pride in their African heritage" and "develop a more positive
self-image as Afro-Americans through identification with the achievements of Africans." The teachers in the three schools represented a
wide cross-section of backgrounds. The teacher in P.S. 197 was a
black American female; the teacher in P.S. 175 was an African male;
and the teacher in P.S. 192 was a white American male.

The purpose of the Harlem study was twofold. First, it was to
ascertain whether black children, who were better informed about
Africa after nine months of instruction, regarded Africa or Africans
significantly differently from those never taking such courses. Second,
the study hoped to find whether any of the goals or the objectives of
the programs, which were to improve self-image, identification with
Africans, appreciation of African heritage, and the development of
ethnic and cultural pride, would be expressed by the students in either
the written responses or taped interviews. On the basis of the responses from fifteen classes from the three different Harlem elementary schools, there was no indication that children who appeared to be
better informed or had more information were more approving or expressed a higher frequency of socially approving sentiments toward
or identification with Africans or Africa.

A total of fifteen classes in all were interviewed, nine from P.S.
197, six from P.S. 175, and two from P.S. 192. This was the largest
number of classes that could be covered during the three-week period
the author was able to spend on the project, primarily due to the
scheduling of the one-hour sessions at various intervals in the three
schools. After written interviews, the author returned to hold tape-
recorded discussions with several classes concerning some of the
written responses the children had made. Excerpts from the tapes
related to such course objectives as identity, racial pride, and other
topics. These dialogues, which were related to concepts that were
also stated goals of the course, provided insight into how certain
attitudes toward self, race, community, and society were formed
and why they continue to persist. Parts of these discussions have
been included to help the reader better understand the reasoning processes and the kinds of factors that influence the responses of black
students who accept or reject Africa or Africans.

The data obtained in the three case studies reveal that after
having been exposed to African heritage classes for nine months,
many students were found to express the same hostile beliefs and
negative stereotypes generally held by uninformed or misinformed
persons. The study also uncovered little variation between brighter
and slower classes, except that the slower classes were less

articulate in their denunciation or approval and less prone to present evidence to support negative or positive opinions. All of the children participating in the survey had been exposed to a nine-month learning experience designed to improve their self-image, help them develop an appreciation of their African heritage, and identify culturally with their African background and heritage. The feelings the children expressed in response to all three questions varied dramatically from class to class and from one child to another within the same class, as the written response and dialogues reveal.

The perceptions, images, and concepts expressed were occasionally objective, often negative, and frequently inaccurate and distorted. Yet these remarks represent more than the childrens' imagination or a test of their ability to recall or accurately describe impressions or facts taught about the people of Africa. These remarks characterize the attitude formation processes that take place during the period in which American children become oriented toward the values, beliefs, knowledge, and opinions of the dominant white culture. These values provide the basis for judging the worth of other people and cultures from a white Anglo-Saxon Protestant perspective.

DISPELLING STEREOTYPES

Many of the attitudes expressed by the black American public school students toward Africans can be seen as culturally learned responses that, except for the discussions of Africans in school, they had never been called upon to use. In the interviews, students in several of the classes were asked if they had ever discussed or talked about Africa before coming to the heritage class, and the responses were overwhelmingly no. Most of the students didn't even discuss what they learned about Africa in the classroom outside of school. However, students were aware of a number of places in their neighborhood, other than school, that were sources for learning about Africa. Among those mentioned by students were movies, television, libraries, after-school centers, community organizations, churches, cultural clubs, speakers on street corners, and Africans who lived in the community.

The images and impressions of Africans black students received through the entertainment media might not be considered functional—since they don't become incorporated as part of the students' formal organized learning experience—but they were, nevertheless, extremely influential. Despite the fact that most black students seem able to make distinctions between Hollywood's fictional entertainment and reality, these images, which are mainly general stereotypes portraying Africa as a jungle and the people as primitive, seem to survive as patterned ways of thinking ready to influence the students' responses if an occasion such as our interview arises. The origin and nature of their expressions of hostility and disapproval toward Africans must be understood and exposed if teachers really expect to help black students overcome these stereotypes, which are obstacles to intercultural understanding.

IMPROVING BLACK SELF-IMAGE

It has often been asserted by sociologists that group differences are in some way involved in the establishment of traditions of prejudice. A group has to be set apart in some way in order to be discriminated against. In the case of Afro-Americans vs. Africans, one of the differences is obviously not color but rather customs, traditions, and values. Pointing out cultural similarities between Africans and Afro-Americans was the approach used by the Harlem schools in its attempt to establish an educational program in which identity with Africans by black students was also presumed to lead to a better self-acceptance, increased ethnic pride, and personal security within a nowly defined black community that is seen as culturally distinct from white America. Even the Harlem public schools were apparently willing to reorganize the African identity of black children as part of the American experience and on equal terms, at least in definition.

The most obvious drawback in this approach to self-image improvement was revealed in the study: the rejection of Africans as well as their culture and customs by black American students in the fifteen heritage classes. To a large extent this may have been due to the fact that by the time those students got to the fourth grade they had internalized the traditional, biased, white American outlooks toward any persons who behave differently from the standards and values they had already assimilated during their previous years in school. In the case of Africa this bias had less to do with color than it did with status symbols and western concepts of success and progress that are at the very core of the American value system.

The conclusion drawn from the case study of the Harlem schools is that many black children perceive themselves as Americans first and hold the same biases and hostile attitudes toward persons of different cultures as do white students. Based on their perceptions and attitudes toward Africans, which in many cases are not seen to be any different from those of white students, there is no reason to assume that African studies should or should not be taught to black children as it is to white children, using the same rationale for the objectives and goals, namely, to bring about a respect and appreciation among Americans for persons of diverse ethnic backgrounds. Such an approach would at least take into consideration the very real distinctions between Africans and Afro-Americans. Public schools might then be able to concentrate on the creation of an awareness of how the superficial and arbitrary distinction, that is, color, has created social problems between black and white people in America. This approach could more easily accomplish the goals of elementary black studies programs than the present unrealistic and unsuccessful attempts to have black children disregard the very real cultural distinctions between Africans and Americans of African descent in an attempt to instill in them ethnic pride as the first step toward self-respect. It may very well be necessary for black children to take pride in themselves first and learn to respect people from different cultural backgrounds second. Educators must understand that only a small part of the history of the African continent is directly relevant to the Afro-American experience.

APPROACHES TO DISPELLING PREJUDICE
AND STEREOTYPES TOWARD AFRICANS

"African Mythology" is the title of an article written by Susan Hall in the publication Are You Going to Teach About Africa?[4] She begins the article by asking teachers, "What picture comes into your students' minds when they hear the word Africa?" She also suggests it is the picture of a "Dark Continent" and all that phrase entails. Although Susan suggests that it is hard to believe that in our scientific age myths about Africa are still being perpetuated, she examines ten of the most popular misconceptions, some blatant, some subtle, to help teachers see what truths, if any, lie behind them. The stereotypes listed as most common were the following:

1. Africa is mainly a land of sweltering jungles.
2. Large numbers of wild animals—lions, leopards, elephants—can be found roaming all over, but especially in the jungle.
3. Africa south of the Sahara is mainly peopled by Bushmen, Pygmies, and Watutsi.
4. Africans have never achieved a high level of civilization on their own or Africa has no history until its discovery by Europeans.
5. Africans constantly engaged in fierce tribal wars before the coming of the Europeans. In fact, it was the presence of Europeans that stopped the Africans from killing one another.

6. Africans lived in primitive villages with no political system; or all Africans lived in tribes headed by powerful despotic chiefs.

7. African men buy their wives and most men have more than one wife.

8. Traditional Africans worshipped many gods or had no religion at all. Periodic human sacrifices were deemed necessary to keep evil spirits from harming the people.

9. It was during the time of European colonial rule that Africans learned about democracy.

10. Tribalism is the most divisive force in Africa today.[5]

Since many of the reasons students in the Harlem study listed for not wanting to visit Africa could be categorized as one or several of these misconceptions, it might be helpful for teachers to begin the teaching of Africa by attempting to dispel these stereotypes. This of course requires a knowledge of some facts pertaining to each of the stereotypes about the continent—facts provided by Susan Hall in her article. The first three notions on the list were the ones most commonly referred to by the black students at the three elementary schools, yet, in spite of the fact that many students held negative or hostile attitudes or beliefs about Africa, the question, "Is there any place in Africa you would like to visit?" was responded to affirmatively by 285 out of 357 students. However, it can be stated that neither negative nor positive impressions influenced decisions to visit or not visit since the stereotypes and misconceptions that were listed in the responses of students who were not interested in visiting Africa were often not much different from those presented by students who wanted to go. In any case, it appears that students wishing to visit Africa and those afraid to would have been disappointed if they knew the truth.

The following responses of the children from the Harlem elementary schools in response to the question, "Is there any place in Africa you would like to visit; if no, why not?" are indicative of the stereotypes Susan Hall described as prevalent among Americans. The facts concerning Africa, as condensed by Susan Hall, are also listed under the responses:

Stereotype: "Africa is mainly a land of sweltering jungles." Student Responses: Reasons for Not Wanting to Visit
P.S. 192
I think that it is too hot.
P.S. 197

They do awful things in the street, and it is extremely hot there.
Because they have snake lions tigers apes too much jungle.
I would not like to visit Africa because in the wild parts, there are
   too many diseases.
Fact: Most of the continent is savanna or grassland while only about
1/7 of it is rain forest.

Stereotypes: Large numbers of wild animals—lions, leopards, ele-
phants—can be found roaming all over, but especially in the jungle.
Student Responses: Reasons for Not Wanting to Visit
      P.S. 192
I would not like to go to Africa because of animals.
Because of the poisonous and dealy animals in the Congo.
      P.S. 197
I wouldn't like to go because I'm afraid of wild animals, I'm also
   scared of savages.
I would not like to visit Africa because it is to hot and in some
   parts of Africa there are wild animals.
      P.S. 175
I would not like to visit Africa because when you can get you can
   get killed, you can get bite by a snake or you might run in to a
   wild elephant and they can run you down or a tiger.
Because there are tigers, lions, camel giraffes to kill you.
I'm get lost in the woods. A lion mete bite me.
To many flys and ants.

Even the students who expressed an interest in visiting Africa often
had similar impressions:

Student Responses: Wanting to Visit Africa
      P.S. 197
I would like to visit Africa because I see the wild anilimd play the
   lion I would bring a monkey home with me and a large elephant
   home with me.
I would like to see lion, monkeys, birds. I would like to play Africa
   drums. I can play drums very good I can play Africa drums.
I would like to visit Africa years ago if I could go back in time to
   the Jungle where I could see a tiger or jaugar and make a nice
   soft rug to play on but, I wouldn't do that to a tiger if I wanted
   because he would have a dinner before I was finished.
      P.S. 192
I would like to visit Africa to learn more about the people. I want
   to see some of the places we learned about like to see statues
   and wild animals. What they at work how they look.

69

I would like to visit Sudan because there are a lot of lions there.
I would like to go because I like animals and Africa had many
animals and I like animals and the people.
P.S. 175
I would want to visit Africa because I like the animals. Some of
the animals like lions, goats, bears, cuts, tigers, seep, ducks,
robins, and I hate Gorrilas apes and vulchers bats, rats, fox,
dingos, eagles, snakes, monkeys, and I'm scared bats and wild
apes.
I think it is a buaiful place to go you do not have to were shoes. It
have grass to see the animals. To catch the animals. To eat the
animals. To like the animals.
Fact: Most of the game animals that are found in Africa live in the
grasslands, more specifically in parks set aside and preserved, often
as tourist attractions, on a small percentage of the land, mainly in
southern and east Africa.

Stereotype: Africa south of the Sahara is mainly peopled by Bushmen,
Pygmies, and Watutsi.

Although the Pygmies and Watutsi were not mentioned by name,
a large number of responses under the category, "Things remembered
about the people of Africa," made references to long or tall people
and to very short people. The following comments from the children
of P.S. 175 in response to the question, "What are some of the things
you remember about the people of Africa?" are indicative of the kinds
of impressions that are the first to be remembered by young children
when people of Africa are mentioned:

P.S. 175
I learned that in Africa there are short people, long
people and all kinds of people in Africa.
Africans are very tall and some are very short and also
some Africans like to dance and the men like to play
drums and sing African song.
They do great things for their country. . . .
They way they work, look, and some of them are very
small and very tall.
They are friendly and they are our ancesters. . . .
. . . They are our ancestors. They have beautiful
clothes. . . .
People from Africa are doing the same thing we're
doing. . . . They wear beautiful jewelry.
The people in Africa have very beautiful clothes, and
they have beautiful jewel. Some people in Africa are
very tall and some are very short.

. . . The Niolites are the biggest.
Some people are short, some are tall. Some are beauti-
     ful.
I remember that people from Africa are tall.
Some are black, some are small, some are tall, some
     are african story telling.
They were dancing and they are different and they do
     not get much money and as much food. Some are
     very tall and some are so very short.
Some are short some are long.

Fact: Why is it that when Americans think of
Africans, these people (Bushmen, Pygmies, Watusis) are
pictured? The total population of Africa is estimated to be
over 300 million people in 1970. Of this number about 260
million live south of the Sahara; included in this figure are,
at the very most, $1\frac{1}{2}$ million Bushmen, Pygmies, Watutsi
and people related to them in physical characteristics and
life style. Also included in this number are, at a low
estimate, 5 million white Africans or people of European
origin who claim Africa as their home.

THINGS MOST FREQUENTLY MENTIONED
ABOUT THE PEOPLE OF AFRICA

General Impressions of African People

This question was designed to have students present, in an
open-ended response, the first general impression the term "people
of Africa" brought to their mind. Figure 1 is an attempt to categorize
the open-ended responses of the 282 students who participated in the
survey. The first column is the class number. The classes were
designated by their room numbers. Four-312 was the fourth-grade
class assigned to room 312. The first column gives the total number
of students in the class at the time the survey was conducted. The
second column is the total number of nonclassifiable responses, and
the third column refers to the number of respondents who gave classifiable responses. This last category included any legibly written
complete sentence in the space provided for answers on the questionnaires. Nonclassifiable responses were blank spaces in which the
phrase "no answer" was typed on the summary of responses; other
nonclassifiable responses were "I don't know" or "I don't remember,"
or incomplete sentences, for example, "The people of Africa."

FIGURE 1

Impressions of Africa
Facts Recalled

	P.S. 175				P.S. 192	
	4312	5308	5309	5310	4228	56301
Total in class	20	26	22	21	31	28
Nonclassifiable resp.	4	1	—	3	7	4
Number responding	16	25	22	18	24	24
Tribes	1	1	2	—	6	—
Cities or countries	16	8	2	4	6	6
Personalities	—	—	—	1	2	3
Products, natural	7	18	—	—	5	2
Dress	5	3	4	5	1	5
Language	4	—	—	—	—	1
Customs	—	1	1	1	—	1
Ceremonies, rituals	1	—	3	3	5	5
Singing, dancing	—	3	5	2	2	—
Tall and short people	4	11	7	2	2	1
Modern dress	—	2	—	—	1	4
Don't wear shoes	—	—	2	2	1	1
Africans are poor	2	1	—	1	—	1
Look, act, dress different	2	3	2	9	14	7
Are black people	4	2	10	1	1	—
Savage, uncivilized	—	—	—	—	3	11
Favorable descriptions	6	4	2	—	4	2
Food	2	—	1	1	—	1
Clothing	5	5	4	5	—	1
Shelter	—	2	—	—	—	—
Hunt for food	—	—	6	2	—	—
Jungles	—	—	1	—	1	—
Live in huts	—	2	2	—	—	1
Many wild animals	—	—	—	1	—	2
Modern conveniences	—	—	—	—	2	1
Stores, hospitals, bldgs.	—	—	—	—	—	1
Occupations	—	—	—	—	—	—
References to ancestors	1	4	3	—	1	—

FIGURE 1 continued

				P.S. 197					
4203	4213	4237	5217	5218	5219	6221	6225	6227	Total
24	15	18	25	18	23	15	21	27	334
—	9	8	1	10	4	—	—	1	52
24	6	10	24	8	19	15	21	26	282
—	1	—	2	—	—	—	—	2	15
7	12	4	9	4	13	3	5	13	112
1	2	3	1	—	—	—	1	—	14
2	—	—	—	—	2	—	1	2	39
9	—	2	8	5	9	9	1	8	74
4	—	2	5	2	2	1	2	1	24
2	—	4	2	1	—	3	1	7	24
1	—	2	2	1	2	4	—	7	36
—	—	1	1	—	—	1	2	1	18
1	—	1	—	—	—	—	—	—	29
3	—	—	8	—	2	5	—	9	34
1	—	1	1	—	1	5	2	—	16
2	1	—	10	—	1	4	—	—	23
5	1	3	3	3	6	1	—	4	63
5	—	—	—	1	2	3	—	4	33
—	—	1	2	—	—	4	—	1	22
—	1	—	—	2	—	—	—	—	21
—	—	2	2	2	—	1	—	1	13
9	1	2	2	—	9	9	1	8	61
1	—	3	4	—	—	—	1	2	13
—	—	2	2	1	1	1	—	3	18
—	—	1	3	—	1	—	—	1	8
1	—	1	—	—	—	2	—	3	12
1	—	1	—	1	—	4	—	1	11
2	—	1	4	—	3	1	—	1	15
—	—	1	3	—	1	2	1	2	11
—	—	2	2	1	1	1	1	—	8
3	—	—	—	—	1	—	—	3	16

AFRICAN IMPRESSIONS

Number of Respondents—282

Number of Responses in Various Categories

112	Cities and Countries
74	Dress (description of people)
63	Look, Act, or Dress Differently (general)
61	Clothing (needs)
39	Products, Natural Resources
36	Ceremonies, Rituals
34	Modern Dress (descriptions)
33	Black People
29	References to Tall and Short People
24	Language (people)
24	Customs (people)
23	Africans Are Poor (general impression)
22	Savage or Uncivilized (general impression)
21	Favorable Descriptions
18	Singing and Dancing
18	Hunt for Food (stereotype)
16	Don't Wear Shoes (general description)
16	Referred to African Ancestors
15	Named Specific Tribes
15	Modern Conveniences (comparisons to U.S.)
14	African Personalities
14	Identified Africans with Black People in U.S.
13	Food (needs)
13	Shelter (needs)
12	Live in Huts (stereotype)
11	Many Wild Animals
11	Stores, Hospitals, and other Buildings
8	Jungles
8	Occupations (comparisons to U.S.)

The selected response categories were chosen on the basis of the items under those categories that children seemed to refer to or mention most frequently. The chart is not exhaustive, as items of minimal frequency were not included. The list of "African Impressions" was compiled from the preceding chart. The impressions listed were ranked according to the greatest number of times that item was mentioned by different students.

The total number of nonclassifiable responses was arrived at by counting the number of students in each class who turned in questionnaires and counting the number of students who failed to give a classifiable response to questions one or two. The highest of the numbers was used. For example, in class 4-312 twenty students handed in questionnaires, two gave non-classifiable responses to question one, four gave non-classifiable responses to question two. Since the frequency of all the items listed on the chart was compiled from responses to questions one and two, the question that had the highest number of nonclassifiable responses was the number listed; in the case of class 4-312 the number would be four. It should be kept in mind that although six questions were really not answered, this represents six questions out of forty, since we are dealing with two sets of questions. There is no felt need to define the results with any more statistical accuracy than has been done, since no test of statistical inferences has been made. In fact, the sample is biased in two respects: first, the lack of random selection and the potentiality of a selection bias occurring; second, the necessity for subjective selection of data, leading to the potentiality of a content bias occurring. The chart and list are merely general indicators of the kinds of responses given by twelve groups of children in public schools after attending classes in which African heritage was taught for nine months in an effort to create certain impressions and attitudes. The objectives of the course were removal of stereotypes, development of positive attitudes toward Africans, and the establishment of identity between the black children who took these courses and Africans. It is clear from the chart that there was no strong positive impact. Finally, there is no way of determining the actual impact the lessons on Africa had, since nothing is known of the impressions or attitudes of the children prior to entering the course. Nevertheless, it would be safe to assume that the courses had very little effect if we hypothesize these existing attitudes being the same as when the students entered. In that case the course failed to affect the negative stereotypes. One would hate to think that the children entered with favorable impressions and left with these impressions.

Of all the things that were shown or said about the people of Africa in class during a nine-month period, many students only recalled the most negative, bizarre, or exotic. In P.S. 192 the following responses are examples:

They have many relious beleafs. They eat animal raw.
The people in some parts of Africa don't wear clothing like the
    pygmies.
They wear some kind of cloth and wrap it around themselves. And
    the way they make bowls with clay and then they let it dray in
    the sun. And that they eat something that doesn't tastes that
    good. But I forgot what its called.
Some of the people wear rings in their noses.

Other students in the same classes seemed to strain in order to be
more objective:

They are very good builders. They are very good hunters. They are
    very good dancers.
The languages they speak are different. They all do not live in jungles,
    forests, and are not savages like they sometimes show us on
    T.V.
That in Africa people are nude and they don't mind. But in America
    there ashamed to walk around nude.
I remember that most African carry things on there heads for good
    posture. Most of them had fruit on their heads.
They are very civilized but still some places are uncivilized.
They are nature loving and believe in traditional customs.
The way they look are not bad to them but to some other people they
    might think its very bad to be running around in a piece cloth.
    But this there culture. So let them do it.

On the other hand, American social and cultural values were used as
the standard for judging African customs, traditions, and progress,
as is evident in the following responses:

That people in Africa wear normal clothing like we do here and that
    they don't wear those rags. I have also remembered that they
    are very civilized otherwise, they wouldn't be able to make
    buildings like we do.
They have different custom. Ugly to them. Is pretty, pretty to them
    is ugly.
We learned about great kings and kingdoms. We learned also that
    Africans are civilized like us.
Africa is not a continent of savages and headhunters. Its a very
    civilized. As a matter of fact its very much like New York at
    least in some places are.

In P.S. 175, which had an African teacher, there were a number
of approving comments about Africans in three of the four classes
interviewed at that school.

They are very clever.
I learned that African people smart.
African people are clever and nice because they are black like us and
    they help us in some ways.
African people are clever, some speak swahili and some speak English,
    some speak both. If you go there to visit they help you take
    your bags to where you want to stay.
They made drums and wooden sculptures of goods and of famous
    people.
They do great things for their country.
They are friendly and they are our ancestors.
I learned that Africa had produced many things that white people know
    nothing about.
People from Africa are doing the same things we're doing. They wear
    beautiful jewelry.
People in Africa have very nice skin and clothes.
Most of the modern dance's come from Africa.

The chart shows that none of the children in P.S. 175, which
had an African teacher, ever used the term savage or uncivilized
when referring to Africans. These concepts were not as effectively
dispelled in class 5-6-301 of P.S. 192, where eleven of the responses
used the term uncivilized or savage either in referring to Africa or
in making comparisons between Africans and Americans. Of the
twenty-one favorable descriptions of Africa, twelve of them, or over
50 percent, came from P.S. 175. However, in class 5-310 of that same
elementary school with the same teacher, of twenty-one responses to
the question about things remembered about people of Africa, none
could be considered favorable. In fact, the very general impressions
expressed by over one-third of the class were unfavorable comments
similar to the following:

They wear funny clothing and look funny.
Africa people look funny.
I think that the people in Africa ware different kind of clothes because
    they are dressed in half clothing.
They dress funny. They look funny because they ware noses.
Africa look funny. They dress funny because they eat funny.
What I remember that the people where queer cloths and they have
    paint on there faces.

P.S. 175 also had the highest number of students who identified themselves with Africans or Africa. Only 16 of the 282 children referred
to Africans as ancestors, and 8 of these were from three classes,
5-308, 5-309, and 4-312, in P.S. 175 that had an African Teacher.
Figure 1.

African people are clever and nice because they are black like us and
    they help us in some ways.
They are friendly and they are our anceters.
They are our ancestors. They have beautiful clothes.
The people are very cultural to us because the people of Africa are
    large and small and medium. The people of Africa are our
    forefather and our ancester.
I like Africa people because they is my color and they like me and I
    will like them.
They is black and beautyful. I am proud those black people. And they
    like they black people.

In P.S. 197, which had a black American woman teacher who wore
African dress to class most of the time, there were 187 written responses from eight classes. Of these, only four comments might be
described as making identifications between Africans and Afro-
Americans:

They are very much like us. Some of them have an English accent.
Some of there people wear torn sheets and some wear clothes like us.
They nice, they are the same kind of people. They land is the same.
That some of the thing have eating come from Africa our home coun-
try.

Apparently one of the objectives was not met, namely, having black
children identify with Africans. Indeed, many of the comments from
the children in P.S. 197 seemed to stress the distinctions between
Africans, who were referred to as "they" and themselves, whom they
described as "we" and "us".

They are brown skin. They speak our language, the women wear long
    dresses.
I have been told that people in Africa dress like us sometimes. And
    they wear clothes like dashikia.
The people in Africa wear clothes just like ours except a few people
    wear native coustumes which are bright and colorful. The
    people in Africa like to do a lot of dancing also.
They wear clothes like us. They have building like some of ours.
They make thire head dress 2   For food they kill the anmail. They
    have our weapons. They have there own God.
They do not have buses or trains or cars. They have to walk.
They were different clothes and eat different.
The people in Africa dress like we do but some do not dress like we.
    They go by there customs. They play game like we do.

The people in Africa are happy people the people in Africa wear
daishiki. I don't think the people in Africa are like us because
of there customs they have.
I remember that some African men can marry more than one woman
at the same time and some africans dress like Americans.

Some students overstated or misunderstood facts that were presented in class, as did the following students in P.S. 175 and P.S. 192:

I learned about black people. And how hard they had to work. I learned
that Africa is a big country.
1. I learned that Africa is a large state. 2. Africa do not have
schools like we do. 3. In Africa when a child get 12 the teacher
come and take them away from their parents. 4. And he or she
is between 26 and they will return home.
That Africa is the largest continent in the world. All women in Africa
except children. Africa is over 3 times the size of the United
States.
It's three times as big as the U.S. There are more than 100 countries
in Africa. There are 580 languages in Africa. The first slaves
came from Africa.
Africa is a continent three times the size of the United States. It contains black people. It has deserts and jangles. It has 700 tribes
that speak 700 different languages. It has pygmies, watusies,
and many more. Some live in mountains and some live in forests.
That not all of Africa is uncivilized. People there use what they have.
Grass, wood, mud. Most people dont wear much clothes.

Several students in P.S. 197 and P.S. 175 had misconceptions
that they said they learned in the course:

The three things I learned was that Africa has head hunters, cannibals
there who scalp you and cut off your head. There is a war in
Nigeria with the Housa Iboa tribe because each wants to be
independent.
I have learned that in Africa there are home like there are in New
York.
I have learned that the Africans can build houses just like the houses
in New York, and they have to catch animals to make their
clothes, and they do not have beds like we do.
I have learned that Africa people dont dress like we do. 2. I have
learned that if a little boy or girl steal something they would
get killed or put in jail. 3. I have learned that some African
people get married in Africa.
Africa is a jungle.

I have learned that Africa is a very small place.

Some students remembered isolated incidents out of context:

People jump rope in Africa.
They way they speak. The way they pick cotton.
A man came from Dahomey to visit our school.
They have police.

In cases where students did have partially accurate information about African society and culture, the value orientation of the students seemed to be toward a negative interpretation of African customs, which were often described as bad manners, uncivilized, or backward. Even students who were objective in their description or made attempts to be fair did not make positive identifications with Africans or their heritage.

There are several possible reasons why most of the students did not identify or take pride in an African heritage, and for the few who did it could be seen that there were factors not related to the content or methods used by the teachers in the African heritage classes. In the first place, many students reported only what they remembered as negative, both from the class and from what they heard the teacher or persons in films or textbooks report. The other point to be taken into consideration is that they were asked to report only what they remembered and not necessarily whether they believed what they reported or why they believed it. For example, responses such as the following are obviously not necessarily the opinions of the respondent but perhaps the best memory of what he has learned in class.

> P.S. 192
>> They are sterotyped as people running around naked in the jungles.
>> I don't know anything about people from Africa because I did not see any people from Africa.
> P.S. 197
>> I have been told that people in Africa dress like us sometimes. An they wear clothes lik dahikia.
>> I do not remember.
>> I remember seeing on a film strip the people in Africa hunt hunt for their food. And instead of eating a deer or a lion or fish a certain tribe eats stuffed rat with deer meat in a sandwich years ago.
>> I remember in a movie that Africa is very hot in most places and very damp in the swamps. The people dress cool. In

very hot and damp Africa there are people in tribes who
hardly dress at all.
P.S. 175
They wear funny clothing and look funny.

On the other hand, many similar comments from students expressed
as statements of fact might probably be retracted under questioning.

A third category of responses is that in which children interpret
what they say using their own value orientation to describe the significance of the African experience. Some of the remarks were patronizing:

P.S. 192
The way they look are not bad to them but to some other
people they might think its very bad to be running around
in a piece cloth. But this there culture. So let them do it.
That people in Africa wear normal clothing like we do here
and that they don't wear those rags. I have also remembered
that they are very civilized otherwise, they wouldn't be able
to make buildings like we do.
P.S. 197
They don't always look ragedy and messy. Some are dressed
like people in New York. Some of them where dahiki's.
The women in Africa carry their baby's on their back. And
the Africans work hard for their childrens food. Some of
the Africans clothes look like rags and they have a dark
complexion.
I remember that some people of Africa are civilized and other
people are like savages. Some people aren't rich enough to
own cars so they ride bikes to work.
Their customs, the way they dress towles and sheets.

THE PROBLEM OF BLACK IDENTITY
AND WHITE CULTURAL ASSIMILATION

Cultural or behavioral assimilation is described by sociologists
as a subprocess or condition in which a minority culture group changes
its cultural patterns to those of the society. I have already referred
to some of the attempts by prominent and well-known black citizens
who were leaders in organizations that reemphasized aspects of
traditional African cultures. Such attempts have been unsuccessful
among the majority of black Americans, but according to one sociolo-
gist, Milton M. Gordon, the extent to which black people have adopted
the cultural patterns of the host society varies by class. E. Franklin

Frazier, in the Black Bourgeoisie,[6] suggests evidence that middle-
and upper-class black people frequently overconform to middle-class
standards of behavior in religious observances, in dress, in sexual
behavior, and in child-rearing practices. The acculturation process
is virtually completed for this group, according to Frazier and others.
These people are felt to be products of life in the United States and
nothing more. How then can the public school reconcile its role as
the major instrument of cultural assimilation and, at the same time,
advocate a separate identity for black students? What could the logical
consequences of such an ambivalent process be for the students with
a low tolerance for ambiguity. The results seemed often to be very
clear cut, an outright acceptance of black to the point that white becomes ugly or, on the other hand, a total rejection of black Africanism
and a denial of African heritage, identity, or even ancestry. As an
example, in one fifth-grade class, the students claimed they could tell
the difference between Africans and black Americans, mostly by
speech and dress.

When the author attempted to point out how difficult this might
be if speech were not included and the dress were the same, the following dialogue ensued. The author first turned to a very dark girl whom
the class agreed looked like an African girl in one of the pictures they
had seen:

Giles:	(To Sharon.) Let's say you were walking down the street in Liberia and there were a lot of other African children there and you were walking, would anyone be able to tell that you were not an African?
Sharon:	No.
Giles:	Why not?
Sharon:	'Cause I'm not.
Giles:	No, wait now, you say that they would think you were an African, right? Why would they think you were an African?
Sharon:	They would think I'm not an African.
Giles:	Oh, they would think you're not. Oh, you think you look different from an African and everybody would know right away? Is that it?
Sharon:	Yes.
3rd Girl:	Only way they could tell I'm African is if I looked like them.
Giles:	Do you look like an African?
3rd Girl:	No.
Giles:	Does anybody in this class feel they look like an African?

Class:	(Long pause. No hands raised.)
Giles:	Nobody? Okay, so then in other words there is a difference you feel.

(Later Giles showed the same students a picture of Sekou Toure.)

Giles:	This is Mr. Sekou Toure; he's from Guinea. (Pause.) Have you seen people with hair like Mr. Toure?
6th Boy:	Yes.
Giles:	Does your father have hair like that?
6th Boy:	Yes.
Giles:	Anybody else in this classroom have a father who has hair like this or who has an uncle who maybe has hair like this? (Pause). Or a brother?
2nd Girl:	My uncle.
Giles:	Your uncle has hair like him?
2nd Girl:	Yes.
Giles:	What color is your uncle's complexion?
2nd Girl:	Darker.
Giles:	Darker? Do you think your uncle might be mistaken for an African if he went to Africa?
2nd Girl:	Yes.
Giles:	All right, then your uncle looks like an African?
2nd Girl:	No.
Giles:	(Laughing.)
Class:	(Laughing.)
Giles:	Okay, we've gotten as far as we can, as far as African identification is concerned.
Teacher:	(Interrupting surprisedly.) When you try to reason about that they cut completely off.
Giles:	Yes, they do. They just turn off.
Teacher:	I wonder why? (Very surprised.) They just seem to freeze.
Giles:	Well, that's one of the things we're exploring.

In an article that appeared in the September-October edition of Africa Report entitled "African Studies: 'The assumptions may be false,'" Leon Clarke, education editor for that journal, referred to the above dialogue and arrived at the following conclusions, which are in the author's opinion quite plausible:

In his dissertation Giles comes to the obvious (and perhaps predictable) conclusion that most black children in his study "perceive themselves as Americans first." He also concludes that the heritage program failed in its stated goals.

After nine months of study, these children seemed to have more information about Africa, but this information did not erase stereotypes. It did not develop positive attitudes towards Africa. It did not help these students to identify with Africans. And presumably it did not enhance their self-esteem.

Giles goes on to suggest that such programs may be asking the schools—and the children—to do the impossible: repudiate years of socialization that has made these children "products of the United States and nothing more."

"How then," asks Giles, "can the public school reconcile its role as the major instrument of cultural assimilation and, at the same time, advocate a separate identity for black students? What could the logical consequence of such an ambivalent process be for the students with a low tolerance for ambiguity?"[7]

These are examples of children with an identity crisis resulting from the confusion created by a school system that cannot really accept black children as Americans and cannot influence them to accept themselves as something else. Thus it stands to reason that two of the most infrequent references on the written questionnaires were to African ancestors, mentioned by only sixteen students in six of the fifteen classes, and to identifications of Africans with black Americans, mentioned by a total of fourteen students in ten different classes.

In P.S. 175 the remarks of one class can be seen in Figure 1 to be so unlike the comments of the three other classes in the same school taught by the same teacher, who is an African from Sierra Leone. I felt it would be informative to hold a taped interview with that class in an attempt to find out some of the reasons for their disparaging remarks about Africa. Although the taped interview did little to contribute to my understanding, it did provide a forum for the students to verbally restate and reinforce their written rejections. These students (an all-black class) refused to be classified as either Afro- or African Americans, refused to be called black, and went so far as to deny having an African appearance. This kind of behavior is obviously in response to factors their teacher should have been aware of before preparing any lessons to help them appreciate or develop a respect for their heritage.

Besides the average ability level of a class, another factor that should be considered by teachers trying to influence attitudes is how bright or dull the students in a class happen to be. Often classes in lower-income neighborhoods were found to be grouped according to

how bright or dull students were. This is probably necessitated by
the fact that almost all of the students in such schools were retarded
in basic skills, so other criteria for organizing classes were necessary.

In some classes where children were unable to read or write
well, they did express a considerable amount of concern about the complex social, political, and economic realities confronting their neighborhoods. A discussion on such matters could be easily encouraged
among brighter students, in spite of language limitations, primarily
vocabulary and infrequent discussions of such issues outside of school.

Interviews conducted in classes with students who were on the
average duller revealed that much of the dialogue with these students
was never above the level of expressing general impressions and
stereotypes. These stereotypes were fixed before coming to school,
and if they were challenged logically, the only result was confusion.
For such students, stereotyping was an effective substitute for real
thinking.

In class 5-4 of P.S. 175, after a class discussion that ended with
a consensus among the students that Africans are always dancing, the
following dialogue took place:

Moderator:	What else do Africans do besides dance? Have you seen them do anything else?
1st Girl:	Make flowers.
1st Boy:	They go hunting.
2nd Boy:	They march.
2nd Girl:	Tell stories.
Moderator:	Very good. What else?
3rd Boy:	They go fishing.
4th Boy:	They cook.
5th Boy:	The women carry babies on their backs.
6th Boy:	They kill animals.
3rd Girl:	They sing.
4th Girl:	They sew.
5th Girl:	House building.
Moderator:	What kinds of houses?
7th Boy:	Straw houses.
Moderator:	Do they have other kinds of houses?
8th Boy:	I don't know.
Moderator:	He's not sure.
2nd Boy:	Brick houses.
6th Girl:	Farming.
Moderator:	We've mentioned all the things they do, now are these the things that we do?

Class:	No.
Moderator:	We don't do any of those things that were just mentioned?
1st Girl:	Some of them.
Moderator:	Some of them, but we don't do all of them? Here's a young lady who wants to answer. What's your name?
2nd Girl:	Carolyn.
Moderator:	Carolyn.
Carolyn:	We don't carry our babies on our back.
Moderator:	Anything else they do that we don't do?
3rd Girl:	We don't kill animals.
Moderator:	What don't we do? We don't kill animals? All right, anybody here eat meat? Who? Who eats meat? (To a boy with hand raised.) You eat meat? What kind of meat do you like?
1st Boy:	Pork chops.
Moderator:	Pork chops. Anybody know how we get pork chops.
1st Girl:	Off a cow.
Moderator:	Off a cow? Everybody agree with that? (No response.) Everybody agree?
2 Boys:	A lamb. (More voices.) A lamb.
Moderator:	Any more answers? Pork chops, where do they come from?
3rd Boy:	A pig.
Moderator:	Pork chops come from pigs. Everybody . . . (pauses to talk to one boy shaking his head in disbelief.) You look surprised.
4th Boy:	(Shakes head in disagreement.)
Moderator:	You don't believe it? (Boy still shakes head.) Well, you look it up later on. Pork chops come from pigs. Now, how do we get the pork chops from the pigs?
1st Boy:	Kill 'em.
Moderator:	Who kills them?
1st Boy:	The men who go hunting.
2nd Boy:	The hunters.
Moderator:	All right, who had pork chops yesterday? (To a boy with hand raised.) You did? Where did you get them?
5th Boy:	From the store.
Moderator:	Okay, you didn't get them from the hunter though, did you?
5th Boy:	Huh?
Moderator:	Do you think they hunt for pork chops?
1st Girl:	No.
6th Boy:	(In background.) They hunt for pigs.
Moderator:	They hunt for pigs, huh?

6th Boy:	They hunt for animals like deers and all that.
Moderator:	Where? Here?
6th Boy:	No, out in the country.
Moderator:	Wait, I think maybe we're getting confused. Some of the Africans hunt for food and others go to stores the way we do. Did you learn that? (No responses.)
Moderator:	Do you think that they have stores in Africa?
Class:	(Several voices.) No.
Moderator:	What pictures did you see, which countries do you remember in Africa? Come on . . . Who wants to tell us the name of one country in African, any country?
1st Boy:	Asia.
Moderator:	In Africa? Anyone know what Asia is? (Pause.) He's close, because Asia is something like Africa, maybe that's why he got it mixed up. (To class.) What is Asia?
Class:	(Voices in Background.) A continent.
Moderator:	A continent! Right! And what is Africa?
Class:	(Several voices.) A continent.
Moderator:	Okay, another continent. Anyone know the difference between Asia and Africa? (Long pause.)
1st Girl:	(Guessing.) Um, Asia is a large place and Africa is not.
Moderator:	Well, how large is Africa? You don't have to give me the exact measurements, but if you were going to compare Asia to Africa, how large would it be?
2nd Boy:	Africa is a dark continent and Asia is not.
Moderator:	Well, it's been called the dark continent. We'll get to that maybe, but what about the size?

The reactions of this class to questions on social identity reflected an unawareness on matters related to ethnic classification consistent with their general overall awareness.

Moderator:	Does anyone know what we call people whose ancestors came from Africa?
1st Boy:	(Softly.) African Americans.
Moderator:	Shout out! Come on!
1st Boy:	(In louder voice.) African Americans.
Moderator:	African Americans! Are you an African American?
1st Boy:	(Shakes head gesturing no.)
Moderator:	Shout out! Come on!
1st Boy:	(in loud voice.) No!!
Moderator:	(To another student.) How about you, are you an African American?

2nd Boy:	No!
Moderator:	How about you? (Pointing to different students.)
3rd Boy:	No!
4th Boy:	No!
5th Boy:	No!
Moderator:	Anybody here an African American?
6th Boy:	Yeah. (Pointing to Mr. Taylor, the African teacher.)
Moderator:	Mr. Taylor? (Laughing.) All right, now why is Mr. Taylor an African American?
7th Boy:	He came from Africa.
Moderator:	Okay, he came from Africa, but Mr. Taylor was born in Africa, right? So that means that Mr. Taylor is not an African American, but something else. Who knows?
1st Girl:	African American.
Moderator:	No. (To Mr. Taylor.) You're not an American, are you Mr. Taylor?
Mr. Taylor:	No.
Moderator:	Mr. Taylor's not an American.
1st Boy:	African.
Moderator:	Right! Mr. Taylor is African. Right. Everybody look at Mr. Taylor. If Mr. Taylor didn't tell you that he was an African, would you be able to tell he was an African?
Class:	(Several students.) Yes.
Moderator:	Why?
2nd Girl:	'Cause he talks like an African.
Moderator:	'Cause he talks like an African? Anything else? Suppose Mr. Taylor never said a word and just came in the room and walked around, looked at you, and walked out. Would you be able to tell he was an African then?
Class:	(Mixed responses.) Yes and no.
Moderator:	What would you think he was?
1st Boy:	American.
Moderator:	How many people have seen people around their block Mr. Taylor's color or about the same color as Mr. Taylor? Who wears clothes like Mr. Taylor?
Class:	All hands raised.
Moderator:	Everybody!! All right, now this is the question, how can we tell the difference between Africans and Americans if we don't hear them? And if they wear the clothes we do?
2nd Boy:	You can't tell the difference.
Moderator:	All right, he says you can't tell the difference.
3rd Girl:	By their color.
Moderator:	All right, Mr. Taylor . . . isn't he the same color as some of the people in our neighborhood? (Pointing to

	student who made first comment.) I think most of us would agree with him. He says that you can't tell the difference unless they speak or they tell you. If they dress the same, without speaking, and they were walking around, you wouldn't know the difference. Now how many agree with him? Okay, everybody seems to . . . (Looking at one girl who didn't raise hand.) You don't agree?
3rd Girl:	No.
Moderator:	You think you can tell an African anywhere you see one?
3rd Girl:	Yes.
Moderator:	You think so, huh? Now how would you tell if they didn't speak and they wore the same clothes?
3rd Girl:	(Remains silent. Pause.)
Moderator:	You just think you could though.
3rd Boy:	The way they look.
Moderator:	The way they look? How does Mr. Taylor look? (Long pause.) Huh?
3rd Boy:	He looks like he's African.
Moderator:	He looks like he's African? Does anybody else in this class look like they're African? Look around.
3rd Boy:	No.
Moderator:	No? No one? Does anyone in this class feel that they look like an African and that if they went to Africa someone might say,"Oh, here's an African girl." Anybody?
3rd Boy:	Sharon.
Moderator:	You said Sharon! Who's Sharon?
3rd Boy:	(Points to a very dark girl.)
Moderator:	(To Sharon.) You Sharon? Okay, Sharon, if you went to Africa and you were walking down the street in a country . . . What's a country in Africa that you know?
Sharon:	I don't know none.
Moderator:	Oh, come on, you remember one. Oh, come one, any country.
Sharon:	I don't know.
Moderator:	Okay. She doesn't remember. Who wants to name a country?
1st Boy:	Egypt.
2nd Boy:	Liberia.
Moderator:	Let's say you were walking down the street in Liberia and there were a lot of other African children there and you were walking, would anyone be able to tell that you were not an African?
Sharon:	No.
Moderator:	Why not?

Sharon:	Cause I'm not.
Moderator:	No, wait now, you say that they would think you were an African, right? Why would they think you were an African?
Sharon:	They would think I'm not an African.
Moderator:	Oh, they would think you're not. Oh, you think you look different from an African and everybody would know right away? Is that it?
Sharon:	Yes.
3rd Girl:	Only way they could tell I'm African is if I looked like them.
Moderator:	Do you look like an African?
3rd Girl:	No.
Moderator:	Does anybody in this class feel they look like an African?
Class:	(Long pause.) No hands raised.
Moderator:	Nobody? Okay, so then in other words there is a difference, you feel.

Compare the above responses with those of another class of fourth graders in the same school that had also been studying about Africa for nine months at the time of the interview under the same African teachers. First they were questioned to determine their awareness and impressions of their own community. One of the problems frequently mentioned was that of dope addiction, to which children responded with suggestions of what they felt to be the causes and also proposed solutions.

Moderator:	What about the black people in America today? Now that they are not slaves, how is life for them, how do you think life is?
1st Girl:	They have to work for other people.
1st Boy:	Bad, because white people talk about 'em like dogs.
2nd Girl:	Because they live in dirty buildings.
Moderator:	You live in a dirty building?
2nd Girl:	Yeah! Everybody else knows I do.
Moderator:	Everybody? Does everybody live in a dirty building?
Class:	(Shouts.) No! I don't. I don't. Not me.
Moderator:	What keeps the buildings dirty?
3rd Girl:	Like dope addicts come in the house and things and they stay around there.
Moderator:	Have you seen dope addicts?
2nd Boy:	(In response to first question.) The tenants, the tenants.
Moderator:	Are you a tenant?
2nd Boy:	Yeah!

Moderator:	All right, she has another problem, she has dope addicts in her building.
Class:	(Voices in background.) I do too, we have dope addicts on the roof.
1st Boy:	I have a junkie in my building.
2nd Boy:	Yeah, and they go behind the stairs and they pee.
Moderator:	The dope addicts?
1st Boy:	I have a junkie in our building, he lives in apartment 12A.
Moderator:	How do you know he's a junkie?
1st Boy:	Cause he always carries bottles and he makes mistakes and he throws them up and he drops them in the hallway sometimes.
Moderator:	Well, this sounds . . . (Interrupted by other students.)
2nd Boy:	And he got a messed-up wife.
3rd Boy:	And he be singing on the steps.
Class:	(Laughter.)
Moderator:	Is this neighborhood a good neighborhood to raise children in?
Class:	(Loud response.) No!!
Moderator:	Why not?
1st Girl:	Because they can get hurt.
Moderator:	Children can be hurt, do you think that children can be hurt?
2nd Girl:	Yes.
Moderator:	When you grow up would you want to live here and raise children?
Class:	(Unanimous response.) No.
Moderator:	Nobody?
	(No positive response.)
Moderator:	Are there a lot of dope addicts in this neighborhood?
Class:	(Large response.) Yes!!
Moderator:	Everyone here knows about that?
Class:	(Several voices.) I know a dope addict, I know a dope addict. (Lots of hands waving frantically to speak.)
1st Girl:	Dope addicts, when you see 'em out on the street they never full, they just, um, bounce up and down.
Moderator:	What makes people become dope addicts?
2nd Girl:	Because once they see someone else doing something, then they gonna go right behind them and try it.
Moderator:	This sounds like a very bad situation. Now I want to ask just one question. Does the school help to improve the neighborhoods?
Class:	(Large number of individual responses.) Yes.

Moderator:	Do you feel that what you learn in school helps your neighborhood become better?
1st Boy:	It can help it become better, but some people don't follow the rules.
Moderator:	Do you think that when you come out of school this neighborhood will be better if you do something?
Class:	Yes! Yes!
Moderator:	What do you think you can do to make the neighborhood better?
2nd Boy:	Run for President, beat everybody up that are dope addicts, and beat everybody up, run for President, put 'em in jail. I'd have the jailhouse full, boy! All them people be coming home, look wife, look wife, boy we got the jailhouse full, wife, look at all the money we got for filling up that jailhouse.
Moderator:	Are there any rich people in this community?
Class:	Yes, yes.
3rd Boy:	(In response to first question.) I would stop selling glue.
Moderator:	You would stop selling glue? Why?
3rd Boy:	Because people sniff it.
Moderator:	Which people? People in this school?
Class:	Dope addicts. (Shouts.) And they sniff fingernail polish. (Voices in background.) I know some, and I know something else.
1st Girl:	If you take dope too much, your heart will get bigger than it is now.
Moderator:	Where did you hear that?
1st Girl:	My mother told me.
Moderator:	Do you think that they have dope addicts in Africa?
Class:	(Large response.) No.
Moderator:	Why not?
1st Girl:	Because . . . I don't know.
1st Boy:	They don't sell dope.
2nd Boy:	Because they don't grow it.
2nd Girl:	Because their masters will whip them if they take it.
Moderator:	Who would whip them?
2nd Girl:	Their masters.
Moderator:	Do you think Africans have masters? Who are the masters?
2nd Girl:	Slave masters.
Moderator:	Do you think there are slaves in Africa?
2nd Girl:	Yes.
Moderator:	(To other students.) Do you think there are slaves in Africa?

1st Boy:	Not any more.
3rd Girl:	Only in Biafra.
2nd Girl:	I would rather live in Connecticut.
Moderator:	Do you think that life would be better if you lived in Africa than it is here in Harlem?

This same class was then questioned about their own ethnic identity, and the following dialogue seems to indicate more positive self-concepts than the previous class, in spite of the same negative conditions prevailing in their communities .

Moderator:	I want someone to raise their hand and tell me why studying about Africa is important. Why do we bother to study about Africa?
1st Boy:	I know, 'cause our ancestors once lived there.
Moderator:	Your ancestors once lived there? Everyone agree? (To another boy with hand raised.) What are you going to say?
2nd Boy:	That's the same.
Moderator:	You were going to say the same thing? Okay, what are ancestors?
3rd Boy:	Our great, great, great grandfathers and all of that.
Moderator:	Okay, fine, and all of those people, right? Now what does it mean that our ancestors come from there? What does that mean to us?
1st Girl:	It means that they are our people.
Moderator:	That the Africans are our people? Okay, now are we Africans?
Class:	Yes.
Moderator:	(To one student.) Are you an African?
1st Boy:	Yes.
Moderator:	You are? (Surprisedly, then to another boy.) How about you?
2nd Boy:	Yes.
Moderator:	You are? (Turning to a girl.) How about you?
2nd Girl:	(Shrugs shoulders.)
Moderator:	She's not sure. (To 3rd Boy.) How about you, are you an African?
3rd Boy:	Yes.
Moderator:	You are an African (pointing to 4th Boy, with hand raised), yes?
4th Boy:	Nope.
Moderator:	You're not an African? What are you?
4th Boy:	I'm American.
Moderator:	American! (Turns to boy shouting "I know.") Yes?

5th Boy:	I'm not African, I'm Afro-American!!
Moderator:	Afro-American. Okay. There's another word we haven't had yet. How many children here feel they are Afro-Americans?
Class:	(All hands go up.) Me.
Moderator:	Everybody! Everybody here an Afro-American? Wow! (Surprised.) Is there anybody here who is not Afro-American?
	(Boy points to the white teacher sitting in the back of the room.)
Moderator:	Okay, the teacher, Mr. Seidman (laughing), right. Okay, now this question. What does the word Afro-American mean? Somebody want to tell us what that means? And how do you know you're an Afro-American?
1st Boy:	Because it's my color.
2nd Boy:	'Cause I'm black.
Moderator:	All right, now that's a different thing; besides an Afro-American, there's somebody who says he's black.
2nd Boy:	(Shouting.) Black is beautiful. (In background.)
Moderator:	What is it?
2nd Boy:	Black is beautiful! (In loud voice.)
Moderator:	Where did you learn that?
2nd Boy:	Every place!
Moderator:	You know that? For a fact? Okay, are you black?
2nd Boy:	Yes.
Moderator:	(To another boy.) How about you?
3rd Boy:	Yes.
Moderator:	(Pointing to different children.) You?
4th Boy:	Yeah.
1st Girl:	Uh huh.
2nd Girl:	Nope.
5th Boy:	Yes.
6th Boy:	Yes.
7th Boy:	Yes.
3rd Girl:	Yes.
8th Boy:	Yes.
9th Boy:	Yes.
Moderator:	Wait, everybody here feels that they're black?
Class:	(Unanimous shouts.) Yes!!
Moderator:	Is there anybody who is not black? Who does not feel that they're black?
Class:	(Background voices shout.) Mr. Seidman. (Pause. No dissenting voices.)
Moderator:	Okay, now then let's move on to some of the other questions. Does anyone remember what the people in Africa did?

Obviously teachers must take into consideration the differences in students resulting from differences in perception, attitude, and response to racism and oppression, as well as their level of ability reflected by mastery of basic skills. In other words, inability to read or write is obviously not the crucial determinant in developing a suitable ethnic studies curriculum for students in all-black neighborhoods from low socio-economic backgrounds.

Conclusion: to try to develop an appreciation and meaningful discussion of Africa's resources and the importance of imports and exports among fifth-grade children who don't know where pork chops come from is to disregard a basic teaching principle, namely the need to begin where the learners are. A fundamental understanding for society and community in which they reside is a prerequisite for making meaningful comparisons and contrasts with other societies and cultures. In addition, the negative aspects of their communities should not necessarily be viewed as an inherent handicap. Although the social and economic conditions, which are the same for all 'disadvantaged" children, may not change anytime in the near future, however, the difference in the way these conditions are perceived by the children could be the first step in helping them rise above the negative influences.

It appears that none of the facts the students learned helped them become accepting of Africans or of themselves as descendants of Africans. Such a negative response was not evident in any of this teacher's other three classes, in which students not only listed favorable impressions of Africans but made written references to their African ancestors and identified black people in the United States with black people in Africa. The only consistent item between this class in relation to the other three in the same school was that none of the students in any of the classes in P.S. 175 used the terms "savage" or "uncivilized" when referring to or comparing Africans with Americans, although a variety of demeaning terms were used to describe Africans by class 5-310, terms such as "looking queer," "wearing funny clothing," and "looking funny." Interesting also is the fact that in response to the question, "Is there any place in Africa you would like to visit?" fifteen members of the 5-310 class replied yes, two did not reply, and only five answered no.

Finally, perhaps most indicative of the extent to which these students have assimilated the American culture is one of the responses by a fifth-grade student in P.S. 175 who wants to visit Africa "to see the witch doctor in Liberia," and states he feels "it's [Africa] a nice place to visit" but "wouldn't want to live there," because they do not have Kellogg's Cornflakes." Thus in considering influences outside of the classroom that affect perceptions and attitudes toward Africa, besides Hollywood, Madison Avenue, and Television, might also be added the Kellogg Company of Battle Creek, Michigan.

NOTES

1. Ethnic Studies in the New York City Public Schools. Bureau of Curriculum Development, Board of Education, City of New York, Project No. 5008, December, 1970, p. 2.
2. Ibid., p. 44.
3. Ibid., p. 2.
4. African American Institute, Are You Going to Teach About Africa? (New York: School Services Division, 1970), p. 12.
5. Ibid., pp. 12-20.
6. E. Franklin Frazier, Black Bourgeoisie (New York: The MacMillan Company, 1957).
7. R. H. Giles, "Images of Africa," "Black and Ethnic Studies Programs at Public Schools," vol. 2 (unpublished Ed. D. Dissertion, University of Massachusetts, 1972) pp. 109, 110.

BLACK STUDIES IN
SELECTED HIGH SCHOOLS

CASE STUDIES: SEPARATE COURSES IN
BLACK STUDIES AT SELECTED HIGH SCHOOLS

While examining the black studies programs in twenty-five
school districts throughout the country, the author found that educational settings, that is, characteristics of the school district and the
student population, had a definite effect on the impact of the program.
That is, certain problems encountered in any specific black studies
program seemed to occur similarly when certain characteristics of
a certain school and community were also present elsewhere. For
that reason, this section of the study has isolated ten situations in
specific educational settings as case studies for in-depth presentation.
Each situation is categorized according to the peculiar context in
which it occurred, and the concerns and attitudes expressed by students, parents, teachers, and administrators are felt to be representative of the concerns and attitudes confronted by persons in similar
roles in other programs observed where the educational settings
were similar. These case studies include separate black studies
courses taught in predominantly white schools to white students,
separate black studies courses in both traditional and experimental
predominantly white schools to black students only, separate courses
in minority studies for white students, required black history courses
in all-black high schools, integration of black studies into the regular
school curriculum in all-black high schools serving a ghetto, black
studies programs in predominantly black high schools serving a middle-
class black community, a white teacher of black history in an all-black
high school, and controversy in the community over a book ruled obscene that was used to teach black studies in an all-white high school
in an all-white community.

CLEVELAND, OHIO: SEPARATE
BLACK STUDIES COURSES FOR WHITE STUDENTS
IN A PREDOMINANTLY WHITE SCHOOL

This brand new building with a heterogenous student population of 2,200 serves a section of the city with a high impact of poverty. Fourteen percent of the students come from families receiving public assistance and 30 percent of the children are from families that migrated from Appalachia. There are almost 400 children with Spanish surnames, many of them Puerto Rican. There are also American Indians, Orientals, and a large percentage of European ethnic minorities. The new school, which opened a year ago, combined two high schools that formerly served the area. The school is located in a predominantly white urban renewal area that contains many multiple low-cost public housing units as well as many private homes that have been neglected. The approximately 100 black students comprise less than 5 percent of the school population.

There is a black history course that has been conducted since the school began. In the first year the enrollment for the course, which is an elective, was so high that four sections were opened. The maximum number of students in a section is thirty-five. The black history course is one of two other electives offered by the social studies department. The other two are current history and social and economic problems.

The teacher of black history taught two sections in black history and two sections of American history in the spring 1972 semester. He is one of five American history teachers at the school and the only black teacher in his department. There are four other black teachers and one black administrator.

Aims and Objectives of Course

The course, which is open to all students in the eleventh or twelfth grade, has no entrance requirement or prerequisite; it is described by the teacher as attracting a heterogenous grouping of mostly white students with varying levels of ability, attitudes, and interests.

The teacher is aware of the eighty-nine-page teaching guide published by the Cleveland School District but chooses to develop his own teaching objectives and topics for his units based on characteristics of the student population that he, the department chairman, and the principal feel are unique.

His classes are predominantly white with a high percentage of Puerto Ricans. He rarely gets more than four black students, which, he believes, is partly because many blacks feel they know what the course is about and partly because he does not present an adequately militant viewpoint. One of the features he takes into consideration in preparing the content for the course is the ability of the poor white students to fully understand the causes and effects of the migration of blacks from rural areas to northern centers and the social consequences of the rise of ghetto conditions and their impact on the ghetto black residents.

The teacher notes that in spite of the ability of the poorer white students to empathize with the conditions of black people in poor neighborhoods similar to theirs, there is less sympathy for them as a group than one might imagine. He feels this is largely due to the attitudes of their parents, who often make comments to his students on the topics he presents in class when his students discuss them at home. One student is reported to have stated his parents' opinion on Adam Clayton Powell, who was discussed in a unit on Black Political Strategies, as being a Communist, not really working in the interest of black people, and in fact, not really a black person but more of a white opportunist.

The teacher engaged the class in a discussion on these points and found that in an open discussion, in which the black students had very little to say, several of the white students attempted to examine and explain Powell's position among themselves. Although they were not necessarily supportive of Powell's cause, most refused to condemn him as a subversive or as insincere. The question of color was also raised, some issues in that area were clarified, and Powell was accepted by the class as black.

The teacher, while in his second year, stated that the main objectives of the course are to help students truly understand the status and conditions of the black man in America from 1619 to the present, something he feels the courses in American history ignore. He feels that course objectives that attempt to go beyond that and portray racism as evil might very likely make a black teacher suspect in the eyes of the white students, whom he "respects . . . for their sincerity" and who might feel they are being persuaded to accept people only because it's the right thing. His lessons must take into consideration the counter pressure and support for the status quo position they hear expressed in their homes and community, which provides an alternative value system affecting any possible influence the teacher could ever hope to attain through a moral position.

The process he feels most effective in his setting is one that provides knowledge and factual information that most of the parents lack and that the school can provide, thus creating a forum for an objective discussion of current events. He also states that he taught the same course differently to the classes of all-black students in his home state of Arkansas, where he served in the high school as a teacher of American history for five years. He explained that his American history courses are not much different from his black history courses and he makes no distinction between American history and black history in the Cleveland schools. To him, black history is talking about the seldom-mentioned black people in a white society. He feels that black students would also benefit from such courses. He cites as an example the response to a question he posed to a black student in his American history class. The student was asked, "What color was Harriet Tubman?" This was after the class had read a section of a regular American history textbook that did not give Harriet's color or race. The student replied, "White." When he asked why she felt Harriet Tubman was white, the girl replied, "Well, everybody else we been reading about was white." The teacher feels it is important to identify black persons when textbooks fail to.

In speaking of class organization, he prefers heterogeneous ability grouping for general courses in black history. However, he felt an honors course for more serious and advanced students would be desirable. Such a course could provide enrichment and more in-depth penetration of certain topics to provide students with an interest or opportunity to become better acquainted with this specific aspect of American history and society.

Administration and Supervision

The chairman of the social studies department says that there are two other teachers in the department qualified to teach black history. I questioned the criteria used by his high school to determine qualifications. His criterion was that persons must have taught or conducted in-service teacher education programs in the area.

The chairman gives the black studies teacher a free hand to order or develop teaching materials, to organize the units of instruction, and specify his own objectives. The teacher of black studies is a part of the regular teaching quota and handles regular American history courses and black history electives. I was informed by the chairman that all history teachers are expected to include the contributions of black people in their American history courses, which all students are required to take. He insists all his teachers include units on black history in the regular history course.

The view of the teacher described above is that including a black studies unit in American history is not enough. If the object of teaching black history or including it in the regular school curriculum is to help the students at the high school, then teachers must be sensitive and aware of the attitudes and reservations resulting from lack of contact with black people, as well as the influence of their local environment and the prevailing social attitudes in the local community. The students are very sensitive on certain issues, and what a teacher says is just as important as the way he says it in these situations.

With regard to qualifications, I asked whether a black teacher would be considered more effective in a black history course in this setting than a white teacher. A supervisor from the Cleveland Board of Education and former principal of a junior high school said that, all things being equal, a person who had lived through an experience he was relating to children would be preferable to a person who had not.

MADISON, WISCONSIN: SEPARATE BLACK STUDIES COURSES FOR BLACK STUDENTS ONLY IN TWO PREDOMINANTLY WHITE SCHOOLS

The black population in Madison has always been very small. In the 1850 census there were six persons listed as Negroes residing in Madison. In 1950 there were 648, still less than 1 percent of the total. Today there is a black community of approximately 2,000 persons according to the estimates of the Madison Public Schools, Bureau of Human Relations. In the 1970-71 school year the Madison school system served a student population of 34,109, of whom 647 were listed as Negro. Of these, 110 were attending the four high schools, where they were less than 3 percent of the student body in all cases. Looking at the high schools, the black population constituted 1.33 percent of the 8,216 total enrollment, and 1.91 percent of the entire school system. I do not believe it necessary to reiterate the effect of social isolation black students experience under these conditions. However, the Bureau of Human Relations of the Madison School System feels that the problem of isolation is heightened by an accompanying absence of black teachers throughout the system. Twenty-five of the city's fifty-one schools have no black or other minority-group teachers, and only seven of the remaining twenty-six schools have more than one. This situation has been described by the Bureau of Human Relations as "undesirable and scarcely tolerable."[1] In a report on multi-ethnic staffing, the Bureau of Human Relations found out, through the results of a questionnaire administered to the thirty-two minority teachers, that even they felt uncomfortable in their teaching environment. The survey revealed that teachers "who were the lone minority teachers in a small white staff felt isolated and in need of other minority teachers to be supportive in that particular school." Against this background we can now review the felt need for separate courses in black studies for black students in two high schools in Madison, one of which, an experimental high school, has fifteen black students out of

an enrollment of 130, and the other thirty-nine black students out of
a student body of 2,224.

Experimental High School

The experimental high school is located on the second floor of
a community center in a predominantly white residential community,
fifteen minutes by car from downtown Madison.
The experiment was funded by the Ford Foundation and was developed as a program of the School of Education at the University of
Wisconsin to provide a facility for the training of urban fellows of
the TTT Program. The school is managed by the Madison Public
School System and there are 130 students enrolled in it, of whom
fifteen are black. Most of the students came because the "traditional"
school setting was not serving their best interests. They viewed a
liberal approach to education as an opportunity for unrestricted growth
and development. The school was described by white students as an
alternative structure for real learning and for informal association
with both faculty and other students. It was felt by the Board of Education that the school would also provide an atmosphere free from the
racial tensions experienced by most of the black students in the predominantly white high schools from which they transferred. The
school coordinator reported that it became evident during the first
few weeks of the school's operation, in September 1971, that a division
along racial lines was mounting in spite of the expressed desires and
attempts of the white faculty members to encourage soical interaction
among black and white students.
The youthful white administrator of the school has the title of
Teacher Coordinator and was appointed by the Board of Education.
He is not an employee of the Board but was hired to run the experimental school on a contract basis and is paid from funds that the
Board of Education receives from the University of Wisconsin, which
manages the Ford grant. On applying for the position he was hopeful
that one of the outcomes of the experiment would be white students'
getting a better understanding of black students through discussion
and interaction on an informal social basis. The introduction of black
studies as a separate program primarily for black students seems
to have hindered rather than encouraged this process. The content
of the courses in the black history program was developed by black
students as part of a special Black Interdisciplinary Program with
goals developed, also by the black students, in response to the following questions:

What is the Black Interdisciplinary Program?
It is an attempt to make an inroad into the predominantly

102

white curriculum (i.e., arts and crafts, yoga, psychology of sensitivity) present in this school.

What is the Purpose of the Black Interdisciplinary Program?
    The purpose of the Black Interdisciplinary Program is to develop psychologically healthy human beings; however, before we can develop to this stage of civilization, we must redefine the Black man in a psychologically healthy framework so that the other human beings —white, yellow, or red—are able to relate to a healthy, self-defined being. In other words, before we can relate to others about us we must learn to relate to ourselves.

Why is the Black Interdisciplinary Program Necessary?
    Based upon the response to questionnaires and interviews on Black curriculum, most of the Black students expressed feelings, without exception (sic), that the present educational structure in Madison is not meeting the needs of Black students.

Couldn't the Same Needs be Satisfied by Broadening the Present Courses of Study at Malcolm Shabazz?
    No. The absence of specific courses related to Afro-Americans or Africans tends to perpetuate institutional racism. The failure of a school to address itself meaningfully to BLACKNESS is the point which evokes criticism.[2]

The need for black studies as expressed by the black students was never conceived as an approach to helping white students better understand the history or culture of their black peers. The black history teacher, who is a black graduate student of history from the University of Wisconsin, is in complete agreement with the goals and the strategy adopted by the black students and feels that the courses in the program, as presently structured, would be of little benefit to white students. The prevailing attitude among the black students seems to be one of wanting to be left alone to think through some of the problems that affect them collectively. For this purpose they requested a study lounge for black students. A large classroom was provided with casual furniture and tables. The room is also used as a meeting room. A sign was put on the door by black students that reads:

103

ROOM FOR BLACK STUDENTS
KNOCK BEFORE ENTERING OR SUFFER CONSEQUENCES
THIS IS A BLACK CONCENTRATED STUDY AREA
ALL BLACKS WELCOME

The Teacher Coordinator received complaints from both white students and faculty concerning the sign and the restricted use of the room. He spoke to the black students and faculty requesting them to reconsider the move they had taken, since it was leading to polarization and, what he felt was worse, many white students who were coming into contact with black students for the first time had come to the experimental school expressing a desire to get to know black students and could not understand the reason or purpose for the action. The black students and staff explained the move as forming a living-learning space where they could feel both comfortable and free from the kinds of racial tensions that had led to their decision to leave their former high schools. The black history teacher explained that the difference between racial tensions in the experimental schools and other schools is that in the other schools they are "glossed over and seldom raised as an issue, but at this school it's concentrated and students not only face it directly but have to share responsibility for reaching solutions instead of just depending on the staff."

Perhaps one of the biggest reasons that the school cannot function as an ideal situation for improving intergroup relations is that Madison is not ideal and the experimental white student population represents a microcosm of the Madison community. The experiment made a deliberate attempt to recruit a cross-section of the population in proportion to racial, economic, and social charcateristics of the larger community. A number of the white students from lower-income families are said to reflect the attitudes of their parents and other members of their segment of the community. In a situation such as this black studies can be seen as a term applied to a variety of topics and courses that black students feel are of interest to them and are needed to "develop psychologically healthy human beings."

Thus the black students felt a need not only for a separate black studies course, but for an entire program, since the new program was not seen to be any more effective at addressing their needs than the one at their former high schools. The second issue arising from the statement of black students is that of separate programs for black students. As can be seen from the statement by black students, the experimental high school is being used to house two experiments. The needs of all of the students seem to be interdependent and mutual. The success of both experiments appears to be crucial if either is not to fail. Failure of either program would invariably affect the other. The significance of the program at the experimental school goes way beyond its original purpose. What is being tested is the need for the expression of cultural diversity within a smaller group that has broken away from a larger group for a reason. The question is will the group of white students now allow the group of black students what they have fought for and won, or are two schools necessary?

Traditional High School

This second Madison school is traditional, with a student population of 2,244, of which thirty-nine are black. Seventeen of the black students are enrolled in a separate course in black studies for black students only. This course was considered necessary because the regular school curriculum was not felt to address the peculiar problems black students face in a city like Madison.

A legitimate procedure for establishing a course for all black students is not spelled out, but white students who applied for admission were told this course was for black students only. The policy of the Madison Board of Education prohibits segregation and discrimination in the public schools and makes no exceptions, yet the teacher, who is black, explained from the outset that the course was being designed and offered for black students only and that only black students would be enrolled. The director of the high school, who must approve all courses, accepted the offering, which was the only course in black history in the entire school. In preparing the course proposal for review by the Director of Curriculum, the teacher stated in the rationale:

> During the past year many of the black students at _____
> _____ were involved in a Community Involvement Program. The students were required to collect service and operational data on the agencies and services in the City of Madison, particularly in their neighborhoods. It was discovered that their inability to collect, organize and analyze data was extremely serious. Their lack of understanding of the institutions which have direct influence on their lives became apparent. In addition many of the black students in CIP had little or no awareness of their cultural heritage, as it relates to the condition of black people in the past or presently. As a result, many of the black students at _____ felt the need for a Community Involvement Program in the 1971-72 school year that would increase their understanding of the institutions that affect their lives and intensify their knowledge of black history.

The course was then reviewed and approved as a community involvement program, but the teacher later changed the title to black studies. The principal stated that all courses in the high school are open to all students, however, he described this course as a pilot program and said if the course were offered next semester it would be integrated and open to the entire school body. The teacher, who is not getting any pay from the Board of Education to either teach or develop the course, is a TTT fellow at the University of Wisconsin who has volunteered his services and who insists the course will remain as it is. The content of the course was described as follows:

> The basic content of the course will cover the period of Africa and the Slave Trade to the current concept of Black Liberation. In addition the course will be designed and taught in such a manner that it will allow for field trips, guest lecturers and parent involvement.

The outline of topics reads as follows:

I. Africa and the Slave Trade
II. The Afro-American Before 1800
III. Slavery in the Nineteenth Century
IV. The Free Black Community, 1800-1860
V. The Civil War and Reconstruction
VI. The Legal Segregation of Free People
VII. The Organization of Protest
VIII. The Great Migration Brings a New Mood
IX. The Depression: Unemployment and Radicalism
X. The Second World War and the Double V
XI. School Desegregation
XII. The Nonviolent Civil Rights Movement
XIII. The Militant Black Liberation Movement
XIV. Black Power Explained

As was mentioned earlier, the course was the only one of its kind, and as can be seen from the topics in the outline, black history or black studies might be considered an appropriate title. On the surface it might appear extremely questionable to have white students excluded from the only course in the school on black history, and perhaps that is one of the reasons the principal is said to have insisted on having the course listed as Community Involvement. The teacher said that he insisted that the name be changed back to Black Studies and was assured by the school administration that credit for black studies would appear on the transcript of the black students enrolled.

It can be seen from the responses of the black students and black faculty at Madison that one of the highest educational priorities for black students is the development of a positive image of self, an identity with the black community, and the fostering of a black consciousness. Black studies are seen as a means to this very essential end. The content and approach of the course, which is historical and cultural, is only incidental. The mere presence of a black authority figure, the teacher, who is interested enough in the black students to guide them through a process of attaining awareness of self through appropriate new perspectives is a unique experience for the black students of Madison. Perhaps the term "black studies" is not appropriate to describe the goals for process and influence of this instructional experience on the psychological and emotional development of the black students involved. Perhaps the question to be raised is, are the public schools an appropriate place for developing this kind of experience? Would the enrollment of white students into sessions such as these impair the goals for black students, for whom the courses were designed? And finally, what benefit, if any, could white students derive from sitting in on "private discussions." If these were considered to be of some benefit for white students, does the benefit outweigh the advantages that black students might derive from an experience of sharing and reinterpreting among themselves their personal, cultural, and social experiences derived from their collective and individual interaction with the white community.

It's hard for black girls to tell black boys how they are affected psychologically and emotionally by seeing them date white girls when the black boys have their white dates in the class during the discussion; there are some things that can be best discussed and better understood when done in private.

White Studies at the Same High School—Minority Groups
in America: A Study of the Courses of White Racism

To view the situation at this school in an even broader perspective one must look at the social and economic stratification of white students. There is a wide variation among the school's student body economically, intellectually, and experientially. This is the view expressed by the teacher of the course in monority groups in America. This course is taught to both white and black students, and the teacher, who is white, feels a need to teach the same course differently to an all-white audience. The school has no tracking or ability grouping system except for pre-vocational students. The course in minority groups, which is an elective, is geared to a broad range of student needs and interests and centers in the courses of racism. The major goals of the course, as explained by the teacher, are to examine institutional racism and examine how the American society has benefited the white middle class to the disadvantage of others and how the system is maintained. The course, being an elective, seems to have appeal to many who are "connected" as well as many who are "curious." There is virtually no way of identifying or reaching the students who really need to look at alternatives to race relations. Even among the curious, students are described as having attitudes that reflect a lack of awareness of what constitutes the problem. Many are described as feeling, "This is just the way things are, the way they always were," and many don't seem to feel a need to question "the way things are."

Making the course required might not address the problem. The teacher feels that the effectiveness of the course depends on who teaches it, what the content is, and how it is taught. He feels that one of the biggest problems in dealing with the topic of racism among white students is that they often become defensive and reactive. He feels that to be effective a teacher would have to "get them to loosen the grip on themselves."

Like the black studies course, the minority group course was developed on a felt need for such a course to deal with the causes of racism that cannot be addressed by black studies or are not being addressed effectively in any of the other courses offered by the school. The teacher of minority groups develops his own outline and content in cooperation with the department chairman. There is no written criteria and the teacher evaluates the students. The course has a format similar to the black studies course in that students are expected to make a proposal to study a specific racial group and develop a project. The teacher prefers to use as case studies incidents that take place in the school, such as how the placement of black children is affected by school I.Q. tests and what the tests represent, comments from teachers about students, and even pictures taken in the school lavatory of signs written on the wall like "Fuck all Niggers," to demonstrate individual racism.

To a large extent both of these courses serve as counseling sessions in which the teachers, who must be very supportive, have to do much more than review history or discuss the problems of racism in a very general academic way. The issue is student involvement, and with most courses of this kind the students who do become involved are often not the ones on whom the discussions are centered. The courses seem to have more appeal to students of liberal persuasion than those who might be labeled racists or bigots. This is the shortcoming of most programs and courses in this area.

DETROIT, MICHIGAN: REQUIRED BLACK HISTORY
COURSES IN AN ALL-BLACK HIGH SCHOOL

The city of Detroit has a school enrollment of 289,587 pupils for school year 1971-72, of these 52,162 were enrolled in the city's twenty-four high schools. Sixty-six percent of the enrollment is black. Several of the eight school regions into which Detroit is divided have majority black populations and several of the high schools have all-or predominantly black student enrollments.

Twenty of the high schools offer separate courses in Afro-American history, one has seven sections, four others have four sections, another has three, six others have two, and seven of the remaining eight have one section each. One school, however, which has a student enrollment of 1,878 students, of whom three are white, has made Afro-American history a requirement and offers fourteen sections. The course is titled Black History I and is required of all incoming freshmen, while Black History II is required of all 10B students. The social studies department has four teachers of black history, all of whom are black. The required black history courses came as a result of student demands in 1968, when radical black students held demonstrations to bring about a number of changes in the school, one of which was the inclusion of black studies in the regular school program. However, requiring all students to take black history did not eliminate the requirement for one year of United States history in grades 10A and 10B. Thus students are now required to take two years of American history, one white and one black.

The black studies syllabus is uniform for all sections and the outline of the content shows that it follows the American History curriculum guide both topically and chronologically. It could be said that the two additional courses in black history are really American history courses from a black perspective. The following topics are the titles of the thirteen units:

    I. Introduction to Black History
    II. African Past
    III. Slave Trade
    IV. Slavery Develops in English America, 1619-1790
    V. The Constitution
    VI. Black Protest Against Slavery
    VII. Emancipation Proclamation
    VIII. Reconstruction and Aftermath
    IX. New Black Leadership
    X. Blacks Who Contributed
    XI. Blacks Organize—Why?
    XII. What Now? Integration/Nationalism?
    XIII. Political Power Now (Black Officeholders)

I questioned why these topics could not have been used to revise the existing American history curricula or indeed why American history could not have been taught from a black perspective and thus meet the city's requirement without imposing the burden of an additional history course on students. I was told that the students who demanded black history did not want a revised edition of American history but rather their own history. Hence, a separate course was felt necessary to respond to this "legitimate" demand. The course outline for Black Studies I is the same as for Black Studies II. The course outline states:

> The main difference between Black History I and Black History II is one of "emphasis." Since the student has a basic concept of the material to be studied, the teacher can now concentrate on details and still have time to teach current events through the oral news reports. Since the class is expected to move at a rapid pace, Black History I is required before a student can enroll in Black History II.

In all of the other high schools black history is an elective, partly because many of the teachers of black history find that black students are concerned more with culture and identification and reject history of any kind per se. In discussing this point with the teachers of black history at the school under discussion, I was informed that the black students involved in the 1968 takeover were students with a vision who were also very much in favor of reform. Many of those students were described, by teachers who remember them, as highly motivated. Now that black studies is required, the inclusion of all students in a heterogeneous grouping has resulted in what one of the teachers refers to as a diluting of the syllabi. An additional problem may soon confront the school with regard to curriculum. The Detroit Board of Education is planning to make a course in ethnic studies at the high schools compulsory, which will mean an additional required course dealing with the history of all minorities. There has been no discussion of a referendum or plebiscite to be held among the current student body to discuss the most preferable status of Afro-American history either as a requirement or an elective. It appears that this high school, like many others, finds itself in the position of having curriculum policies formulated by earlier student demands, which have now become rules with no provisions for review or revision based on consideration of the changing conditions that might make a new approach more feasible. What alternatives are left to students who might see a need for another legitimate curriculum reform? What forum is open to them to voice their opinions and share in the development of their education besides the takeover?

LOS ANGELES, CALIFORNIA: INTEGRATING BLACK
STUDIES INTO THE REGULAR SCHOOL CURRICULUM
IN AN ALL-BLACK HIGH SCHOOL SERVING A GHETTO

Jordan High School in Los Angeles is virtually a ghetto within a
ghetto. Located on 103rd Street, it is bounded on one side by the Jordan Downs housing projects—two-story, ash-gray buildings that contain 2,200 families, most of them on welfare. To the east is Alameda
Street, the border of Watts, and there are railroad tracks on Alameda,
so that when you cross them you know you are entering a different
world.

This description was written by Johnie Scott, a former student
and graduate of Jordan High School who is now a reporter for
Time magazine. In an article in the June 18, 1973 edition of Time
magazine, Mr. Scott compares Jordan High School today with Jordan
ten years ago:

> When we Ameliorants graduated from Jordan, our class
> had average grades of only 1.6 on a 4.0 scale. That sit-
> uation has improved some, to 2.25, but last month Jordan
> still ranked lowest of all Los Angeles schools in achieve-
> ment tests. Some officials say these tests are unfair,
> but others see a difference in the students. "These kids
> come to school believing that academic education is not
> going to solve many of their problems," says one. "They
> are more quiet now because they're searching deeper for
> answers."

The school is one of the two high schools in the Watts district
of the Los Angeles Unified School District. Of the 1,934 students in
Jordan, all are black except thirty-four Mexican-Americans. The
school became almost exclusively black when over 300 Mexican
students left Jordan after an incident of violence between black and
Mexican students in 1968. Most of the Mexican students went to a
nearby high school, which is now over 60 percent Mexican. Fifty-
three of the 101 faculty members at the school are black. There is
one course in black history and the teacher of that course is white.
The chairman of the history department and the principal, both of
whom are black, feel the white teacher is very well qualified to handle
the course.

Many black students disagree, and I was allowed to interview a
class of thirty-eight black students in an American government course
to get their views. One of the students interviewed was the former
chairman of the Black Students' Union. In his opinion, neither the
present white teacher nor the previous black teacher address themselves to the needs of black students. He spoke of the need for a black

consciousness, an awareness of self, and a positive black image. The principal had said of the former black teacher that he had a very good knowledge and background in black history. Yet, the specific criticisms voiced by the black students against the way the former teacher presented the course were concerning his ideology rather than his qualifications. The students who were most critical voiced the following complaints: "His cultural national approach was outdated"; "The course, which was supposed to be a black history course, turned out to be a regular history course. He talked about the depression and topics the students covered in other courses"; "He spent too much time on Garvey and anti-slavery activists and other things in the past without dealing with current problems in the black experience." The former chairman of the Black Students' Union summarized by saying, "He just didn't relate as well as he could have." I asked whether the black students expressed their dissatisfaction with the course to the teacher and was informed that a few outspoken students had been asked to leave the classroom on several occasions after open disputes with the teacher. These were described by the ex-student president as students who complained that the course material was inadequate and who were asking for more relevant discussions.

The present white teacher was criticized as a black history teacher because, as the students put it, "He couldn't be relevant even if he wanted to." Several black students said they also confronted him and others say they have refused to take his course. This is the first year the white history teacher, who has been in the school three years, has taught black history. The students say he admits that there is a problem of empathy, which some say should disqualify him.

The problem of obtaining a black history teacher has been one the school has been struggling with since the demand for black studies was first stressed by students in 1968 and 1969. In spite of the fact that the students initiated the demands, there was never any student input in the formulation of the syllabus or course content. The content and structure of the black history course has always been left up to the teacher. There is an approved outline for the content of that course, as there is for all courses approved for the high schools by the Los Angeles school district. Even if this were followed, it appears the topics covered in that outline would not be any more acceptable to the black students than those the teachers developed themselves. None of the approaches seems to address the sociological and psychological aspects of black identity. The principal stated that since black studies was first introduced, three different teachers tried to handle it but with very limited success. In his opinion none of them lived up to the expectations of the school or the students. I spoke with the present teacher, who is chairman of the history department, and the former history teacher, who is black and now teaching at another all-black school. The purposes of the interviews were to find out what they felt the goals of the black studies programs should be at the school and to what extent they were willing to consider how much the courses could or should respond to the demands of students, namely that such courses help black students identify with a concept of black, develop a more positive self-image, and create an awareness of black identity and consciousness.

The former black teacher of black history is now teaching at another high school, which I also visited. In his opinion the articulate demands expressed by the few students who advocated the course in black history were not representative of the many who took the course. He described many of the students in the courses he taught as not being academically inclined, and quite a few did not even have enough information to "rap constructively." Most of the discussions were based on hearsay. There were also students who were serious about black studies and accepted it as they did other courses. There were others who he felt only used it as a vehicle for involvement, involvement being described as activities taking place at all levels and in all areas, for example, meetings, demonstrations, and protest activities. There were also many different views of black studies among the faculty when it was first introduced. Some responded to the courses as meetings to discuss cultural or ethnic matters of common concern, others viewed the courses as an administrative response to placate the militant fringe, some described those demanding courses as troublemakers. The administration, he alleges, responded to the demands of the student community, which it viewed as a reflection or microcosm of the black community in Watts, which was viewed as active and militant. He also pointed out that many of the students who cried the loudest for black studies never took the courses.

The chairman of the history department and present teacher of black studies is not in favor of separate courses in black studies as an alternative to curricula revision. He feels that among many of the students at the school there is a serious need to develop and improve basic skills and that one of the major objectives of any course in the history department should be to combine content with skill development. He is not as concerned with what the courses are called as he is with the content. For that reason he feels his department has one of the strongest black studies programs in the city, although there is only one course entitled black history. He states proudly that all of the courses that are offered through his department are presented from a black perspective and the teachers, who use the approved titles of the Los Angeles school district, develop their own outline and content based on student needs. In his opinion the real problem with most of the courses that were not taught from a black perspective is that they failed to take into consideration the discrepancy between the value orientation of the black students and the American social order. In the history courses, students are being helped to examine and analyze the wide range of views of the black and white society. This school subscribed to a number of newspapers, magazines, and journals, among them the Wall Street Journal, the Christian Science Monitor, and Black Scholar, which students are expected to read and use to prepare assignments and do research for class. The chairman feels that separate black studies courses as electives are less attractive to black students preparing for college, since courses in political science, economics, and constitutional law are more impressive to college admissions officers. He described his role as one of "bootlegging black studies." He points out that even the courses in international relations and American constitutional law, which he teaches, deal with current issues affecting black people from a black world perspective.

Black Studies in a Predominantly Black High
School Serving a Middle-Class Community

This new high school, constructed in 1968, is located adjacent to a prominent middle-class black community in Los Angeles. The area the school services consists essentially of single-family structures, homes varying widely in value from a $16,455 median in one tract to a $36,395 median in another.[3] The range of housing values reflects a variation in employment status from one section of the high school district to another. Homes in the $36,395 median bracket belong primarily to professionals. These are located in one district in Los Angeles and outlying county areas. There are large groups of unemployed in the less affluent sectors, while the full range of lower-, middle-, and high-income occupations are represented in the others.

The racial make-up of some areas of the community served by the high school is not reflected in the school population. For example, the 25 percent nonblacks in the area do not appear in that proportion in the high school's enrollment. In fact, one particular area of the district has a 40 percent white population, but most of these are older persons with no children of school age. The total enrollment is 3,606 students, of whom 3,527 are classified as black, twenty-three as Oriental, seventeen as students with Spanish surnames, and one as American Indian.

Three other high schools are located in this area of the Los Angeles Unified School District, and of the four the one being described has the largest black population. The school has had a black studies program since it opened. Two sections of an Afro-American history course and two sections of an Afro-American literature course are offered. The Afro-American history course is offered for grades 10-12 as a one-semester course with no pre-requisites. The school also has a black awareness council club, which collects money and food and engages in other social activities to raise funds for needy black families. The administration, which is integrated, describes the student body as having a much wealthier group of students than any of the other all-black high schools in Los Angeles. The school counselors also pointed out that many of their students were exposed to busing and other integrated school plans while they were in elementary and junior high school. Many of the students were bussed out of the area when they attended junior high school and were then eligible to attend predominantly white high schools served by their former junior high schools. The counselors also advised me that most of the students who were bussed out in junior high school chose to attend this predominantly black school upon graduation.

The Afro-American history teacher, who is black, was teaching his first semester at the school. He was formerly at a school in Watts and transferred to be at a school closer to his home. He pointed out a number of differences between the students at the two schools. He also described the difference in his approach to teaching black studies, a result of meeting different student characteristics. His first concern centered on the class enrollment. He claims it is hard for him to believe that out of 3,350 black students only thirty-eight registered for black studies. His feeling is that Afro-American history should be an alternative to American history but that this cannot be accomplished under the present school regulations. He also stated that he teaches American history courses, which he approaches from a black perspective, although he noted a limitation of American history is that it does not allow time to handle the African background of black Americans if the curriculum outline is followed. He feels that more black students should be encouraged to enroll in black history courses, including, but not limited to, those who want to specialize in black history and those who lack a sense of pride.

This teacher feels that one of the goals of black studies courses should be to help students develop a sense of pride in relation to the Afro-American experience and the African struggle for independence. He also feels courses should stress the relationships between the oppressed and the oppressors in the contemporary scene. In connection with this he mentioned what he perceives as a feeling of helplessness among many black students when discussing the lack of achievement among black people in America. He feels that one of the ways to help overcome this negative impression is to point out the achievements of Africans in history. According to him the Los Angeles Board of Education's course outline and materials distributed to teachers for teaching about Africa do not in any way relate to this need. Reviewing this situation he suggests that only teachers can prepare outlines that relate to the needs and feelings of their students and that contain the kind of knowledge and information needed to produce desired changes in attitudes.

He discussed the difference in attitudes between students at his former high school in Watts and at his present high school. His present students seem to have a much broader outlook and perspective and can be more easily encouraged to feel that they will succeed and achieve than the Watts students. For one thing, these students are much closer to success images in the neighborhoods in which they reside, View Park and Baldwin Hills. The black students at the high school in Watts, as a result of the neighborhood and the experience and conditions in their community, were found to be much more lacking in self-confidence. They were exposed to fewer people and situations that could be considered successful by middle-class standards, and this affected their outlook and attitudes toward self, school, and society. One of several examples he cited as a common practice in his present school was students' writing out invitations in class and passing them to friends in school inviting them to attend parties being held in their homes over the weekend. In Watts less entertaining was done in the homes, for obvious reasons, and there was much less social formality. It was also pointed out that there is apparently very little intimate knowledge of the conditions in the Watts community among his present students. The chief source of information for these students is the same as for all high school students in predominantly or all-white communities, namely, the news media, and an occasional person who works in or had had reason to visit Watts. "These kids are just not in the know about Watts" is the way he sums up his impressions, based on discussions between students from Watts and black students from this high school. He is in favor of having the black students from the school make class visits to Watts and meet students there to get to know more about black disadvantaged communities from a firsthand view. For that matter, he feels a major limitation of the students he taught in Watts was their lack of facts about their own and other black communities. He described many of the Watts students as not being academically oriented and therefore very often inclined to use the class for rap sessions. Yet many of these students needed more information than they had, since very few knew facts, therefore much of their discussion was based on and centered around clichés and hearsay.

In the course of my interview a number of suggestions were proposed by the teacher regarding the direction and content of black studies for this high school. These suggestions were based on the experience the teacher had at both this high school and the one in

Watts. In general he felt the background, experience, and ability of the students should determine the kinds of learning activities and the content that each course in black studies adopts. It was in this light that he commented on the limitations of the curriculum guide and the course outline approved by the Los Angeles Unified School District, which all teachers were expected to follow.

His feeling was that this guide and course were inappropriate for both Watts and the present school for different reasons. Many of the students who presently take his black history course are interested in and capable of a more in-depth study of the black experience than is provided by the outline. In discussing this matter he seemed to have the background and foresight to recognize the limitations of the suggested course in relation to the needs and interests of his students. However, the larger problems are that, first, there is no special requirement to teach this course; secondly, in most schools where the guide is used, the teachers of American history who offer this course often have no training or experience and therefore are completely dependent on the materials available in their approach to teaching the course. Thus many students capable of becoming more involved in the learning process are often exposed to a very superficial and unchallenging presentation. Since many of this teacher's students have had exposure to black churches and homes and have schools in integrated settings, he prefers a problematic approach that incorporates and builds on their experiences rather than a straight history lecture. On the other hand, for students who lack exposure and experience as well as basic information, a course such as the one the Board of Education proposes might help provide a description of the problems.

Administrators often ask what kinds of black studies courses would be more appropriate in an "all-black setting." The above description of two high schools with all-black enrollments are hopefully examples illustrating that the term "all-black setting," with no more information than that, has no more meaning than the term "all-white setting." An all-white setting in a low-income area is bound to have social and economic characteristics similar to low-income areas comprised of members of ethnic minorities. On the other hand, black children from homes and communities with middle-class value orientations and aspirations have much in common with their white counterparts. However, one very real difference is the gap between aspirations and expectations, which is wider among middle-class black children than among white students because of the American practice of racial discrimination of which black children are very much aware. Perhaps the psychological effects of prejudice and discrimination should be handled differently by teachers when discussing this social phenomenon among the victims of racism than when discussing it among those who benefit from it, whether or not they favor it. More will be said about this in Chapter 5 under Conclusions and Recommendations.

A White Teacher of Black History in an All-Black High School

This is the first year the teacher of the black history course has taught it at this high school. He has been teaching math at the school for the past three years and is familiar with the mood of the students and understands the social climate of the school and the reservations on the part of some students about having a white teacher for the black history course. In the interview with the teacher we discussed the content and the objectives of the course, the methods, materials, assessment techniques and problems, and his background and preparation for this assignment. He majored in history in college and had been teaching mathematics, for which he is also qualified, at this high school since he came three years ago to fill a vacancy in the math department.

His experience before coming to this all-black high school was in a predominantly white high school in another school district in California. It was during his assignment at the previous school that he developed an interest in learning and teaching black history. In his first year at the previous school he taught American history classes to all white students. That school, which has a 20 percent black population, also had a track system that grouped students in classes according to their ability; most of the black students were block grouped in classes. It was during his first year at that school that black students began protesting the fact that the history courses were not including the contributions of blacks and other minorities, and they demanded courses in black history. Although he had no black students in his class, this teacher felt inclusion of minority groups and their points of view were appropriate topics for his American history courses, and accordingly he developed lessons to include these topics. It was at this point that he began to realize how little he knew and began to read on the subject and investigated courses that might be available at the local colleges and universities. Several white students complained to the administration that his views were too radical and that he had departed from the standard course outline, which they felt represented what they were supposed to be learning. He feels that this incident, in conjunction with his open support of the black students' request for changes in the curriculum, led to his being assigned to teach students in the lower ability group the following year. The next year he had several classes that were predominantly

118

black, which led him to investigate the possibility of teaching black history and introducing new topics. He explains he got into trouble with the administration again, this time over the use of unapproved reading materials and not following the curriculum outline prescribed by that high school and the school district. One of the books he was criticized for assigning was Soul On Ice by Eldridge Cleaver. In his opinion the way in which American history was outlined in the curriculum guide was not relevant for any students, black or white, because it disregarded their needs and interests. However, he found it difficult to convince white students that the regular course was not relevant and, indeed, was limited in its approach. One of the white students in the lower ability group complained that he was favoring the black students in the class over the whites. Meanwhile a course in black studies was approved by the school in response to the protests and demands of black students. However the course was to be taught by white teachers whose view this teacher considered to be very conservative. Further there were only two black teachers in the school, both in the English department, and neither was involved in the protest for black studies, nor did they openly support it as a few other teachers had. The teacher enrolled in black studies courses in the local colleges, but he was not asked to return to the school the following year. He explains his decision to teach in an all-black high school as being based on his previous experience and conviction. He felt he would find this school more compatible than an upper middle-class oriented white school.

The course in black history he is now teaching had an enrollment of forty-eight students when the semester began but is now down to twenty-five. Many dropped complaining that the work was too hard. He encouraged several to leave, among them the athletes, who would have had to miss a number of sessions. The course is an elective open to all grades and there is a wide range of abilities, which, he states, makes a single approach difficult. He has alerted the school counselors to the difficulties many students are having and requested them to program only students who are felt to be capable of doing the work. He has developed his own course outline and says he has never seen one produced by the school district. The major goals of the course, as he describes them, are to develop critical thinking skills, help students examine critically the ideas of persons they read about in class and, hopefully, develop their own ideas. Another objective is to familiarize students with different philosophies and programs for the resolution of racial conflict and for black self-improvement. The problems he faces are in two areas; first, there is the problem of student background and interest. The lack of motivation for children to whom no type of history has any appeal is compounded by the fact that he has not come across any texts that help relate or explain the significance of the past to the present. In his opinion there are no good history texts for the black experience that take into consideration the problems of motivation and achievement. Most of his successful students are seniors who have mastered the basic study skills, that is, reading and writing, which includes knowledge of grammar and composition. A large number of students don't do well in black history, he feels, because they have not been taught to read, write, or think. He feels these skills are prerequisites for his course. The other problem he faces is rejection and resentment by black students from both ends of the political spectrum.

Now that he is in the history department, he also teaches courses in American history. In these he has included several topics from the black history courses. In one of the brighter classes several black girls complained that he was teaching black history when he should be teaching American history, and they left the class in protest. Even among the students who remained, there were those who felt they should be learning American rather than black history. The explanation given by them was simply that if American history was the name of the course, that's what should be taught. Many of them also expressed a feeling of being shortchanged. They had already heard complaints in the neighborhood that the program in their school was different from and inferior to the programs in white schools. On the other hand, many black students refuse to take a course in black history from a white teacher. Yet even among those who do, there are often a few who express open resentment, cynicism, and hostility. He also notes that this appears to be more prevalent among the girls than the boys. The boys seem to either leave or state their objection to his presence and refuse to enroll. The girls who remained seemed more disposed to remain and express their negative sentiments in and outside the class. He remembers two girls in particular who resented the fact that they had a white teacher for black history and refused to participate, although they attended the classes. They both filed but never changed their attitudes or behavior toward him during the entire semester.

The day I observed his class, the lesson for that period was to have been a discussion of Charles Silberman's analysis of the racial situation in the United States. The instructions written on the blackboard were: "Write an essay which explains and evaluates the factors which Silberman believes have caused the current racial crisis." The students had been assigned Crisis in Black and White.[4] He took the first ten minutes to explain how he expected the class to organize their essay. He also stressed the importance of their giving their own opinions. There were eighteen students present when the class began. As he was writing the assignment on the blackboard, several complaints by students could be overheard. One girl commented,

"I don't know nothing about his ideas," another exclaimed, "That book was too hard." As the teacher began to explain the assignment, a boy entered late, sat down next to a girl and began talking to her. The teacher called him by name, told him if he didn't want to do the assignment he could leave but he could not remain and disrupt the class. The boy responded by picking up his coat, hat, and books and walking out. The teacher continued explaining over the grumblings and complaints of a few students. Some students asked to be able to use the book to write the essay. He compromised by allowing them to use any notes they took while reading the book. The discussion of the assignment continued for a few more minutes and students began to take out pens, pencils, and notebooks to begin the assignment.

The teacher is aware of the students' various notions of what black studies is, and I asked his opinion on this. He has noticed that students with a lower level of ability often express a greater need for identity. He guesses that this might be because they feel threatened, embarrassed, or ashamed. He also noted that his notion of black studies is not one that even black teachers can handle effectively. He cites the fact that the previous teacher, who was black and very well informed and in agreement with a need for black studies, was also rejected by many students for different reasons. Finally, without the support of the administration, which is all black and respected by the students, he feels his job would be impossible.

NORTHAMPTON HIGH SCHOOL, NORTHAMPTON, MASSACHUSETTS

Northampton High School is a three-year public high school of approximately 1,000 pupils in the city of Northampton, a small city of approximately 30,000 persons, located in the Connecticut Valley of western Massachusetts. The population of Northampton is predominantly white, and this fact is reflected in the composition of the high school student body, which has one black student. There are black people residing in the area, employed by the four hospitals in the area, one of which is the U.S. Veterans Administration Hospital, which has black staff and patients. The city is also the home of Smith College, one of the largest private women's colleges in the United States, with 2,400 students, of whom 161 are black. There are also 7 black members of the faculty of 240, who reside in Northampton in housing provided by the college. There has been no great expansion of population in Northampton during the past ten years, nor has there been any change in the ethnic make-up of the population. There has been a limited influx of persons of Puerto Rican background, but this has made little impact as yet on the community or the high school. The city remains a white community, as it has been for many years. While there are numerous substandard dwelling units in various locations, there are no clearly delineated slum areas. There are no ghettos, nor are there any large exclusive residential areas. The community could be described as prosperous, but there is no evidence of extreme wealth.

In a Report of the Visiting Committee of the New England Accrediting Association, prepared in April 1970, from which most of the above information was obtained, the faculty of the Northampton High School was described as being in agreement with William P. Channing, who said:

> [Our task] is not to stamp our minds on the young; but to stir up their own; not to make them see with our eyes, but to look inquiringly and steadily with their own; not to give them a definite amount of knowledge, but to inspire fervent love of truth; not to burden their memory, but to strengthen the power of thought; not to bind them by ineradicable prejudices to our particular . . . notions, but to prepare them for the impartial, conscientious judging of whatever subjects may be offered to their decision.

It was perhaps out of a committment to this idea that courses in the area of Black Studies were introduced into the school in 1970.

In its report the Visiting Committee commended the curriculum of Northampton for eighteen specific efforts made by various departments of the school. One was to social studies "for recognizing the need to modernize the program." However, an ensuing controversy over the materials used in teaching the Black Experience courses revealed that there was not complete agreement among the faculty of the high school and members of the community on how to loosen the bind by "ineradicable prejudices to [the community's] particular notions."

This incident reported could have happened anywhere; it has in other communities similar to Northampton. For that reason it was chosen to illustrate potentially controversial aspects related to teaching the contemporary black experience to an all-white audience, middle-class oriented, highly insulated, and culturally isolated.

The Northampton Incident

On a Saturday late in May 1971, the usually slim weekend edition of the Daily Hampshire Gazette marked the beginning of a brief but bitterly emotional controversy among Northampton residents, city

government officials, and school administrators over materials used
in a black literature course taught at the local high school. The newspaper displayed a front-page article entitled "Police Order Book Removed from School," along with a large photograph of the cover of
Manchild in the Promised Land, Claude Brown's autobiographical novel
depicting his early years in Harlem and the major object of the controversy of the ensuing weeks. However, what is also interesting about
the Northampton case is that the suitability of the book for use in the
classroom did not remain the sole issue. The potentially explosive
question of the school board's discretionary power in regard to the
content of the curriculum and the equally troubling question of the
rights and prescribed duties of the police both fell under critical examination in the course of the controversy and led to many members
of the previously insulated white community becoming aware of some
of the most controversial aspects related to the teaching of the contemporary black experience in America.

The appearance of this broader issue of police vs. school power
was sparked by the manner in which the controversy became known
to the press and to the public: several "concerned" parents complained that they objected to the "indecent" language in Manchild (which
was currently being used in a junior-senior elective English course
at the high school) to the police—rather than to the school board, the
body that routinely handles such complaints. (The parents much later
claimed that they had appealed to the School Committee for help but
had received no assistance.) This irregularity immediately aroused
an undercurrent of suspicion and antagonism.

The first newspaper coverage, mentioned above, consisted largely
of police comment and statements of police intention. The Police
Chief claimed that after having the book reviewed, he had written
letters on the previous day to the Mayor, the Superintendent of Schools,
and the School Committee Vice-Chairman stating that he and his detectives had found 387 "obscene words or phrases" in Manchild (a
list of those words was allegedly enclosed in each letter) and that
unless the book was removed from the high school, he would "press
criminal charges against those responsible for introducing the book
into the school." According to the Gazette, the Chief's letter was the
impetus behind an unscheduled School Committee meeting Friday
afternoon—the same day the letters were received. The Committee
met in executive session with the City Solicitor, and the statement
released by them to the newspaper was succinct and moderate in
tone: the Chief's letter would be considered a "complaint" and would
be handled routinely. The Committee also invited the Police Chief
to a joint meeting to discuss the matter.

Several years earlier the Northampton Public Schools had established formal channels for curriculum review. In this case, the

central reviewing body was the Media Committee, consisting of the Northampton High School librarian and principal, the director of media services, the head of the English Department, and the two teachers involved. The review procedure itself consisted of five preestablished steps. The Media Committee was to:

1. Read and examine materials referred to it;
2. Check general acceptance of the materials by reading reviews;
3. Weigh values and faults against each other and form opinions based on the material as a whole and not on passages pulled out of context;
4. Meet to discuss the materials and prepare a report on it;
5. File a copy of the report with the Superintendent of Schools.

Meanwhile, the Chief continued to insist that "several" parents had complained to him and were now formulating a petition to the School Committee requesting the removal of all the course books. The Chief claimed that the book was "offensive" to him and his detectives and that it was a "pretty rough" book for eighteen-year-old. He also claimed knowledge of several students who were ashamed to tell their parents about the books. The Chief was confident that the Northampton schools were in violation of Chapter 272, Section 28, of the General Laws of Massachusetts, which prohibits the distribution of obscene things to persons under eighteen years of age. That law states in part that any material "harmful to minors, meaning that the quality of description or representation of nudity, sexual conduct or sexual excitement which appeals predominantly to the prurient, shameful or morbid interest of minors under 18 years of age; is patently contrary to prevailing standards of adults in the community, as suitable material for such minors, and is utterly without redeeming social import for such minors." The crime is punishable by up to five years of imprisonment and a $5,000 fine.

The Northampton Schools responded by holding a meeting with the City Solicitor, and they quickly began to prepare a legal defense. They released to the newspaper informative material about the black literature course and the system's book selection policy in general. The course in question had been in the curriculum since 1969 and was entitled "Black Literature—Composition I" under the English Department course offerings. The description of the course in the Northampton High School course catalogue reads: "This course will offer the student a very important segment of American literature which has been left out of the curriculum too long. Students will read

selections of autobiography, drama, poetry, short stories and novels
by Afro-American authors including Douglass, Baldwin, Hansberry,
Hughes, Malcolm X and Brown. Throughout the course students will
have the opportunity to improve their writing skills by writing about
remembered past events and present happenings. Student writing will
include memoir incidents, reportage, and journal keeping. Student
reaction to class readings will be a part of their journal keeping."
As stated by the School Committee Vice-Chairman, the school system
has a broad book-selection policy, the purpose of which is to "develop
an appreciation of many racial, ethnic, religious and cultural groups."

The following edition of the Gazette again gave front-page coverage to the incident. The article reported that the city's District
Attorney had that morning filed a request for a show-cause hearing
with the police in District Court in regards to what the newspaper
termed a "potential criminal complaint" against the Superintendent
of Schools, the principal of the high school, and those responsible for
introducing the book into the school. The District Attorney openly
stated that his sympathies were with the school administration. Also
announced in the article was a meeting that was to take place that
day between the Police Chief and the Mayor. The exact purpose of
the meeting was not disclosed, and the newspaper seemed to rely
heavily on the police for comments on the course of the controversy.
The police seemed to have taken advantage of this coverage by creating the impression that they were levying the power and that the
situation was entirely in their control. The Chief stated that he'd give
the school authorities "elbow room" before he took any action, stating
that ". . . we're trying to be fair and reasonable." The Chief also
stated that in his opinion the District Attorney was overstepping his
bounds by acting as a "defense lawyer." "I question his ethics," the
Chief was reported as saying.

The press was not allowed to attend the meeting between the
Mayor and the Chief (two other members of the School Committee
were also present). But what was discussed—or decided—on that Mon-
day afternoon apparently had an effect on police tactics during the
following days. The next day's newspaper carried a statement by
the Chief to the effect that the Police Department would wait for the
outcome of the Media Committee Report before seeking criminal
complaints. The Chief was reported as saying that the meeting was
"very friendly" but "just prolonging the situation" and that his future
course of action would be in "keeping [his] option open if they don't
ban it permanently." The emphasis seemed to shift from alleged
criminal violation, although there was a redetermined insistence to
get Manchild removed permanently from Northampton classrooms.

In the meantime, the Mayor announced that the School Committee
considered the Police Chief as the sole complainant because they had

not received any other complaints from any parent or citizen (the parents who the Chief claimed had spoken to him bypassed the routine channels for complaint and therefore were legally disregarded).

What were the words in Manchild in the Promised Land that had spurred the Police Chief to become, as one enraged citizen said, the "moral arbiter" of the community? As soon as the Media Committee began its review of the book, a number of the words were disclosed: "pimp," "chitlins," "virgin," "oversexed," "hell," and "prostitute." The entire list contained 387 words, one of which was repeated 92 times, another 76 times.

The Gazette carried many letters to the editor during these weeks, many in support of the Police Chief and many vehemently opposed to him. But all the letters had one quality in common—all expressed a concern with the question of who decides what is the proper content of the curriculum and, as in this case, who determines the criteria for judging material "obscene." The writer of one letter in support of the Chief did not specify what she felt were the "indecent" qualities of Manchild, but instead suggested that it be replaced by the works of George S. Schuyler (Black and Conservative, Black No More, etc.). This letter and many others stressed the community control aspect of the issue—parents should have a voice in what their children read because "they are paying for it." In nearly all the letters in support of the Chief, there was expressed a strong mistrust of the School Committee's discretionary power. Many people could not believe that these formal channels could act for the common good.

Fear and anger could also be found in the letters of those opposing the Chief—fear of unwanted and illegal police control. "For Chief W_____ to set himself up as moral arbiter of the community seems an unfortunate misdirection of police energies," commented one woman who insisted that Manchild was of "undeniable social importance" and that its languages was necessary to its message. The bitterly sarcastic letter of a student from Northampton High School suggested that Sons and Lovers, the Aeneid, Volpone, and As You Like It be removed from the curriculum, as they also contained "indecent" language. "I am also happy to see the Police Chief in the forefront of the battle against that corrupter of youth: literature. Long live search and destroy missions," he concluded.

By Thursday, May 27, the controversy had attracted the attention and concern of many persons and organizations outside the Northampton area. The Massachusetts Attorney General, in a speech at a nearby high school, claimed that Manchild "can't be classified obscene by any Supreme Court standard." The Hampshire County Chapter of the American Civil Liberties Union wrote to the Mayor stating its intention to become involved if the police pressed criminal charges. "That any volume of critically acclaimed merit should be banned from the public schools is serious enough, but that banning should take place at the instigation of the chief of police is beyond tolerance," the ACLU wrote. In the midst of all this turmoil, the police chief commented that he would persevere in his legal proceedings against the schools. The letters to the editor that day included one from a black woman who soundly and articulately pinpointed a central issue: white ethnocentrism and the tendency of whites to define "American" only in terms of their own culture-bound values. Academics from the surrounding colleges also began to send irate letters to the newspaper, some demanding the resignation of the Chief. The Five-College Black Student Executive Committee also wrote a letter of protestation.

By the end of the week, more action by groups opposed to the Chief had been taken. Thirteen clergymen from Northampton and surrounding towns met at St. John's Episcopal Church and there composed an open letter to the editor of the Gazette (the clergymen claimed that the Mayor had been present at the meeting and had been supportive of their action; however, the Mayor reportedly denied this when questioned later by reporters). The clergymen's letter insisted that the discretionary power of the Media Committee should not be "subject to legal harassment, intimidation, or intervention." The letter also deplored the parents' use of police tactics rather than of established channels for complaints. Some of the letters to the editor were fervent. One citizen even referred to the Chief as a "moralistic, dictatorial white knight" and condemned the community's "myopic . . . white, middle-class, safe, suburban" point of view.

As Northampton waited for the Media Committee to complete their review of Manchild and to announce their decision, an editorial on the issue appeared. "What is Obscenity?" its title queried. Its content was brief and decisive: ". . . the point that has to be made is who is to decide what is and what is not objectionable," the editor claimed. He concluded that according to the law (which was quoted at length), the Police Chief had no grounds for legal prosecution. The editorial described Manchild as "realistic" and urged its readers to adopt a sensible, unemotional perspective: "Let's give our children some credit."

On Wednesday, June 2, the Superintendent announced that an open School Committee meeting was planned for June 7. Also made public that day were the results of a Northampton High School survey conducted by the Student Government. Two hundred of the school's students responded to the questionnaire, which attempted to measure student opinion of Manchild—97 percent of the respondents supported the use of the book in the curriculum. Not one of the respondents said he was "very much offended," and only 4 percent said they were "somewhat offended." The Student Government survey also suggested ways in which to avoid controversy in the future—by notifying parents of the exact course syllabus, etc.

And, predictably, letters to the editor became more intense as the School Committee meeting grew closer. Supporters of Manchild had over and over again stressed that rough language was necessary to the book and that it was valuable reading for high school students as part of their realistic preparation for the world. One woman, dismissing Manchild as "filth," typifies the frequently expressed retort: "I have lived my life thus far without such knowledge and feel that I am just as well rounded an individual as someone who knows all the sordid details of every segment of humanity." Another common theme in many anti-Manchild letters was a conception of (high school age) children as unthinking, automatic imitators of all they read. Many people simply did not trust their children to read maturely. The fear felt by some persons was obviously based on a concept of their children as valuable property they felt they should fully protect or control: ". . . the most precious possessions we own." This fear was perhaps the impetus of the mistrust of the school administration and the urgency that was so often expressed: ". . . we must take make those decisions for ourselves . . . don't let others . . . ACT NOW !"

The letters also revealed much about the attitudes of some outspoken residents of this middle-class community toward blacks in general. An especially lengthy letter condemned Manchild as "gutter trash," those responsible for its presence in the curriculum as "dewey-eyed, mush-brained intelligents," and Claude Brown as a "racist." The author of the letter concluded by insisting that Manchild is an insult to those black people who are Christian, hard-working, pure of mind, and energetic enough to "get themselves out of the ghetto."

On Tuesday, June 7, only a few days more than two weeks after the beginning of the controversy, the Gazette carried a headline in red: Manchild Back in School; Chief Delays Comment." During the previous evening's meeting, the School Committee, which had the power to overrule the Media Committee recommendation if they wished, voted unanimously to accept the favorable recommendation of the Media Committee Report. (The Media Committee, basically, had insisted that Manchild was of significant social importance and was a valuable experience for high school students.) The meeting concluded without incident. Representatives of the Massachusetts Teachers' Association and the National Teachers' Association were present and promised to support teachers threatened or harassed because of the decision. The Superintendent's only comment to the press after the meeting was "I'm just glad it's over." The Police Chief was not available for comment.

The course on Black Literature was offered again in the fall of 1971, and Manchild was used as one of the readers. However, the description of the course was modified to read as follows:

The themes of oppression, disenfranchisement, the struggle to be an individual, and the search for one's identity
will be explored in the writing of Afro-American authors,
among them books written in the realistic, everyday language of the ghetto, which might be unacceptable to some
readers.

NOTES

1. 1971 Status Report with Recommendations On: Recruiting
and Retaining Teachers and Administrators from Minority Groups.
Human Relations Council, Madison Public Schools.
2. Statement prepared by Black Student Caucus at Malcolm
Shabazz Experimental High School, Madison, Wisconsin, Fall, 1971.
3. 1970 Self-Evaluation Report prepared by the high school for
the Regional Accrediting Association.
4. Charles E. Silberman, Crisis in Black and White (New York:
Random House, 1970).

CHAPTER
5

SUMMARY, CONCLUSIONS, AND RECOMMENDATIONS

WHO SHOULD TAKE BLACK STUDIES?

The Harlem fourth-grade study (described in Chapter 2) was designed to provide knowledge and increase the respect of black children for contemporary Africa, thereby enhancing their own cultural pride and personal self-image through identification with an African heritage. The overall result, after nine months' exposure to the program, indicated that the black children had just as great a tendency to hold negative stereotypes about Africa as did white and black children who were not in the program. There was evidence that the children in these Harlem classes were perhaps better informed about Africa, but rejected Africans just as much as other children who were not included in the program.

The undeniable conclusion is that there are attitudes that permeate deeply into American society and have already shaped the beliefs of elementary school age children, creating a screen of values that all but obliterates the deliberate efforts to teach children to identify with people of another culture. Seemingly these responses come from an American value structure that characterizes people who are different as strange. Thus, the stereotypes of Africa prevail even in the minds of fourth graders who have been differently informed.

The most crucial issue to consider, however, is not merely the elimination of stereotypes but rather the question of the primary goals of Afro-American studies in black elementary classrooms. If the purpose is to promote a strong self-image and pride based on African heritage, then it appears from these data that black children are being burdened with an extra obstacle in being expected to identify with people (Africans) before they have even learned to respect them. Black children, as well as white children in America, are subject to general prejudices and stereotypes toward Africans. This unfortunate bias has resulted in an additional burden being imposed on black children. For them African identity is presented as a condition of achieving self-respect, an obstacle that white children do not experience. The black child in an Afro-American class is expected to develop a positive image of himself through identification, not with his American culture, but with a black culture that is essentially foreign to him as well as to all American children. The public schools should be setting an example by respecting black children for what they are and helping them to respect themselves. Before being asked to accept Africans, black children should first have pride in themselves for what they are, Americans. Schools should be freed from the need to impose African culture on black children as a prerequisite for self-respect. Black children are seen by American society as Americans, not Africans. The goals of the public school should be to help all children understand that similarities and differences are a basic condition of American life and to enable each individual to accept his ethnic distinction as a basis for the realization of self-worth. Self-respect and group-respect should be seen as earned, based on the way people conduct themselves where they are, in their own culture. African culture, when taught to any American child, should be taught as an alien culture. Based on the findings of this and other studies, research provides sound evidence that an alien culture should not be taught to black children any differently from the way it is taught to white youngsters. The Harlem study shows that the black children are saying the same things about Africans that white children are: "They look funny," 'They talk funny," and similar negative comments.

The attempt by public schools to develop racial unity and identification based on color avoids the issue of racism by focusing on problems in areas other than the crucial one: the American Society. This shift in emphasis also avoids the problem of examining the racist attitudes of the creators and perpetuators of a pseudo species called Negro and circumvents an examination of the real differences between Americans, which is not skin color but the results of ownership and control of the means of production which, in the hands of one group, enable it to control and effectively restrain the mobility of another.

This being the case, the only real basis for identification between Americans and Africans is one related to their similar positions and conditions resulting from an imbalance of power in which both are oppressed peoples with common oppressors. An honest approach to black studies in American or African society would reveal racism as the one common institution operative in both societies that has rendered two entirely different groups of people powerless for the same reason.

Courses in Afro-American studies should help all students examine the skill with which racism has been used to oppress the natural progress of black people in America. The interests of American students, white or black, are not served by courses in ethnic or black studies that focus on artificial or superficial distinctions, such as color or ethnic background, designed to create subgroup ethnic identities among children who are in many important ways very much alike.

In many cases schools in the districts visited appeared to be using diversionary tactics, unwittingly or wittingly, by claiming to address the problem of racism through the introduction of black or Afro-American studies. The nature of the historical relationship between black and white people in America suggests that the history of black people is nothing more than a history of the effects of racism. A presentation of this history in no way examines or gives reasons for the causes of racism.

To understand the reasons racism developed and continues to persist in American society will require a revision or perhaps replacement of the present textbooks and curricula used in most public schools, courses and textbooks that give a racist interpretation of the entire history and progress of mankind. What is needed is not black studies or a study of the responses of black leaders to racism, but rather an examination of the motives and the dynamics of the behavior of certain white groups who have practiced racism with the utmost effectiveness. Thus, there is little black studies can do to constructively respond to racism either in education or American society. Black studies as a response to racism, or as a vehicle for establishing pride in or identity with an African heritage, is an inappropriate activity for the public schools and one that has resulted in failure where these have been stated as goals.

This conclusion is based primarily on the observations, discussions, and impressions resulting from the author's visits to twenty-seven school districts in the course of conducting this study. Although this statement does not lend itself to quantitive documentation, I feel there is sufficient evidence in the form of statements by school personnel, students, and others concerned with black studies to warrant this conclusion, based on their experiences.

On the basis of information obtained in the course of this study, there is sufficient evidence to conclude not only that African studies programs are being viewed unrealistically by school districts through attempts to introduce them therapeutically to reduce racial tension, but also that the role of some of the black professionals in these programs in public schools could be called questionable. It might be appropriate to elaborate on the assumed connection between racism and African studies at this point and refer to prominent black authors— who have also commented on the fallacy inherent in the position adopted by black and white citizens—who stress the African past as a means for improving the black image of Afro-Americans. The main criticism is that this focus is often used as an alternative to addressing the real

132

and immediate issues and conditions that impose social, economic, and political restraints that block the natural progress of black people in America.

Obviously the term "black studies" could have as many different meanings as there are courses that bear the name. Black studies has been viewed as the schools' solution for almost all of the problem related to racism in American society. In both the elementary schools and the high schools surveyed, black studies courses were seen by both teachers and students as appropriate forums in which to discuss all kinds of problems related to racism. They incorporated one or several of the following goals: to improve intergroup relations, to provide for the need for a strong self-image among blacks, to develop respect for members of minority groups, to help members of minority groups develop pride in and respect for their heritage, and even to increase academic achievement levels among poorly motivated students. There was often a general consensus as to the validity of these vaguely stated goals, but the development of instructional activities to achieve specific objectives related to these goals was almost always missing.

CRITERIA AND STANDARDS FOR DETERMINING THE IMPACT OF BLACK STUDIES PROGRAMS

It may very well be that the term "black studies" can have no real meaning as a basis for communicating ideas related to a single concept. Undoubtedly many definitions are needed and many alternative program models may be necessary in order to meet specific problems in specific locations.

As school districts consider instituting black studies programs, they must bear in mind the diversity of meanings and purposes such programs are often found to have among different advocates within the same community. Communication of purposes and clarification of program goals is often impossible when all people involved in demanding and planning black studies are not in agreement and hold various diverse expectations that cannot be reconciled through a single program.

Of the several high schools visited, eight were selected as specific case studies, each of which was felt to illustrate a unique but not uncommon situation related to the development and implementation of black studies. In each of these cases, different needs were recognized and different approaches emerged. Almost every combination of teachers and students is represented in the eight schools. For example, in one case there is a white teacher teaching black studies in a school with an all-black administration and a predominantly black student body. In another school the black studies course was taught exclusively to black students, while the white students were allowed to enroll in another course in minority studies. In another case black students were required to take a course in black history that barely differed from general American history, except for the presentation of some topics from a black perspective. It became quite clear in studying the results of just these four case studies that in formulating the purposes of a black studies program the characteristics and needs of the students for whom the program is designed must be identified and used as the rationale for the course objectives.

The development of the course content and the related learning activities will understandably vary from school to school and among classes within schools. Yet there is an evident need for schools to be more specific in spelling out the purposes and contents of programs entitled "Black History" or "Black Studies."

As pointed out earlier, there are a variety of topics and themes related to black studies outside of the history discipline. Many school officials interviewed by the author are in agreement with a conclusion rendered by Dr. Wolfe concerning black studies as a body of knowledge that must be interdisciplinary if it is to have certain purposes.

It utilizes the content, methodology and skills of the separate disciplines of history, sociology, anthropology, psychology, literature, language, linguistics, political science, biology, geography, social welfare, economics, law, theology, music, art and drama but is also interdisciplinary since the Black Experience is interdisciplinary. Certainly, there is sufficient evidence to demonstrate that the traditional disciplines have not been adequate to the task of understanding blacks. Hence "Black Studies" cannot afford the luxury of "hardening the categories" if it is to have the dynamic quality it must possess to meet the following purposes:

1. To build an understanding of the history of Africa and its development with special emphasis upon Black Africa, including a study of government, family and community structure, art, literature and language, music, drama, laws, education, customs, religion, occupations and every aspect of the culture of the people.

2. To heighten awareness of the effect of the migration of black Africans to the Western Hemisphere, especially to the United States.

3. To deepen the appreciation for the contributions of black people to the entire development of civilization.

4. To foster an understanding of the unique "black experience" in America, as it is reflected in:

a) Afro-American modes of cultural expression;
b) Afro-American social and political institutions;
c) Historical developments within the cultural, social, political and economic contexts of American life.
5. To study the problems which Afro-Americans face in American communities today and, wherever possible, actively cooperate with individuals and organizations of the black community in their solution.[1]

In determining purposes and approaches, schools need to examine more carefully the kinds of students who are enrolling in their black studies courses. Who needs the program? Should the focus be on black courses for black students? If classes are designed for white students, which white students are enrolling? Often white students enrolled in black studies courses were described by their teachers as being of liberal persuasion or sympathetic to blacks and had some knowledge of their experience. What about the needs of the other white students as they relate to the broader goals of the school and community? Should black studies courses be required of all students, as they are in some Detroit schools? On the other hand, what changes in content, method, and expected outcomes should occur if all students were required to take black studies? The case studies presented some schools' reasons for separate black studies for black students and revealed some predictable student reactions to such courses when required.

GOALS OF BLACK HISTORY COURSES

If an agreement could be reached allowing a variety of perspectives for a broader interpretation of American history, then a distinction could be made between American history and other kinds of topics included in courses labeled black studies. Black history might then be defined more appropriately by public schools as a branch or part of American history. Then, by describing the scope, content, and intent, all persons interested in the discipline would know what they should and should not expect. Perhaps, then, courses that are felt necessary to meet other needs of white or black students might be more precisely labeled and defined in terms of their specific content and objectives. It may very well turn out that courses in "black studies" that are not part of those in the American history category would require teachers qualified in other disciplines such as, driver, sex, specialized vocational, or religious education. In some cases psychologists or persons trained in human relations might be used to examine concepts underlying intergroup relations and ways to improve them. Community organizers or social workers might be able to help students not familiar with the black community better understand the impact of the social and cultural factors that contribute to the conditions there. Members of civil rights organizations might best explain various strategies as well as political and economic obstacles, with which they are very familiar. Special seminars or workshops might also be organized for black and white students who wish to come together to discuss problems of race either during the regular school day or after school. Finally, other demands placed on the school in the name of black studies might also be considered in terms of their appropriateness as part of the regular school curriculum. It may be that an extension or expansion of the existing curriculum would be necessary to incorporate community and student requests for educational programs, should the school consider them as a legitimate part of its function.

On the other hand, it may turn out that none of the above-mentioned suggestions would be acknowledged as appropriate educational or learning objectives. If the latter be the case, then the public schools would at least be in a strong position by stating it. They would then be better able to define their role as well as their limitations in order to discourage what schools may consider unreasonable demands presently being directed toward the schools and their professional staff. Such requests often expect the public schools to play a role that requires resources and a commitment that neither the policy-making bodies that govern the schools nor the professional staff are able or willing to undertake. If schools were to redefine their role in the area of ethnic or black studies, their community residents and others who are serious about meeting the need for such programs might then expend their energies more productively by engaging in activities directed toward areas from which more positive results might be anticipated.

Another very real possibility is that black children whose parents would like them to develop a black consciousness or awareness-of-self based on concepts of Negritude or other philosophical or religious percepts might find that released time from school—the equivalent of religious instruction, for which there is a precedent—would be a more appropriate and effective approach. The one difference between the demands of black students and community groups and those of other minority groups is that in no case have the Chinese, Japanese, Indians, Puerto Ricans, Mexican-Americans, Jews, or other ethnic groups come to school expecting middle-class value oriented teachers, white or otherwise, to discuss with the members of those minority groups what it means to be Chinese, Japanese, and so on. Granted members of the above groups are persons of well-defined cultures that have customs and traditions that are not often appreciated, understood, or respected in a racist, white, middle-class oriented society where everyone is judged by "American" values, yet the legitimate demands of these other groups have been towards the promotion of cultural diversity in the public schools. They demand that American history be taught in a way that portrays American society as a product of the successive and continuing interaction among theirs and other ethnic and minority groups, beginning with the original inhabitants.

America is a pluralistic society; there should be no questions in the minds of any teacher who understands that concerning the inappropriateness of an educational system that presumes "cultural deprivation" for all whose life style is not white, Anglo-Saxon, and Protestant. Until very recently the role of the public schools was one of persuading nonwhite children to repudiate their behaviors that characterized them as being different. This attempt has taken its heaviest toll, psychologically and emotionally, on the black child, who is today perhaps the most assimilated of any minority group. Since teachers, by virtue of their own education and the selection and recruitment process of most school districts, are still seen as the major exponents of white middle-class values, on what basis should we realistically presume the schools to be capable of helping any children develop an appreciation for the appropriateness and legitimacy of the variety of cultures different students represent? Not even a takeover and management of the schools by the indigenous communities could produce different results if the system remains the same. The schools are a reflection of society.

PROBLEMS RELATED TO THE ROLE OF THE
TEACHER IN THE BLACK STUDIES PROGRAMS

The role of the white teacher in black studies programs at either white or black schools is obviously a difficult one. He is resented by white students of both liberal and conservative persuasions in predominantly white high schools for different reasons and rejected in predominantly black school by both serious black students and those who are more inclined to hold rap sessions. The teacher's training, background, experience and/or commitment, which are in many cases evident, are seldom the issue and are almost never taken into consideration when his removal or replacement is demanded by black or white students. This predicament does not allow for the "all things being equal" approach. In both predominantly white and predominantly black high schools that are recruiting for a black studies course, it appears that often a lesser prepared black teacher is given preference over an equally or better prepared white teacher. However, in discussing preparation, also to be considered is what is often referred to as relevant background and experience related to the content of the course, a factor that without question often enables certain teachers to be more effective if those elements can be incorporated into the instructional experiences provided the students. Although many black teachers have personal experiences related to topics covered in black studies courses, this does not seem to guarantee their effectiveness with black students, as was shown in the case of the high school in Watts.

Perhaps additional formal training would help persons with community experience to utilize it effectively in their lessons; on the other hand, maybe the ability to develop a more effective teaching style based on personal experience requires a sensitivity and talent that colleges that train teachers should consider a prerequisite for becoming a teacher in black or minority studies. Many black teachers in all-white schools resent being used as informants for white colleagues and students whose primary motivation for enrolling in black studies seems to be to find out how it feels to be black in a white racist society. On the other hand if the more formal academic approach used by black teachers is not seen as any different from that of a white teacher, then what are the advantages that black teachers are felt to have that justify them being given preference over white teachers? Unless it is assumed that by virtue of being black they do something that makes the course more authentic, then the premise that "all things being equal, a black teacher is more effective than a white one" would have to be reexamined. This is in fact being done in several school districts where black teachers actually appeared to be more "white" in their approach than some white teachers. On the other hand, the confusion among white administrators when this occurs is often the excuse many administrators need when black students who demand black studies reject the black teacher because of his point of view, approach, or for any reason that has nothing to do with his qualifications. This makes black studies appear to be more political than academic, which, as their study has attempted to point out, is sometimes the case. It becomes virtually impossible to discuss the preparation of teachers for black studies courses or programs when the criteria for an effective teacher include who will be given a chance to teach. In any given school where separate black studies is offered, the decision concerning who teaches will often involve political, administrative, and other kinds of considerations that have little or nothing to do with preparation.

Another problem to be considered is the questionable distinction of the title "Black History Teacher," as opposed to "American History Teacher." At present there are no stated criteria or qualifications in most school districts to teach black history in any other ways than those required of teachers of American history. However, in special

cases, a person who is not qualified as a history or social studies
teacher in some school districts can obtain a certificate of competency
that allows him to teach black studies in public schools without proper
teaching credentials. Thus an American history teacher is allowed
by most school districts to teach black studies with no formal or additional preparation or experience, but a person acknowledged to know
American history well enough to teach the black experience will often
find himself restricted to teaching just that subject and usually limited
to presenting it to audiences of all-black students.

A LARGE PART OF THE SOLUTION LIES IN
TEACHER PREPARATION

The most direct approach to the problem of curriculum revision
rests with the institutions of higher education that are responsible for
the training and preparation of future teachers. These institutions
currently exercise a weeding-out process of persons who resist or
refuse to "successfully complete the process of teacher education."
To most college teachers of American history there is only one United
States history. United States history from a black perspective, black
history, or any kind of history other than that which the colleges have
continued to present for the past fifty years, is dismissed or suggested
as an appropriate course for the black studies program or department,
but is not considered to have any scholarly or academic validity.
Often history majors will not receive history credit for taking courses
in the Black Experience or Afro-American history. The colleges and
universities have handled the teaching of black history in a very separate and unequal manner. Separate courses and programs in black
studies or Afro-American studies have been instituted in most colleges
and universities in response to the demand of people deploring the
inadequate treatment of minorities in existing history courses. The
creation of separate courses for the interested few has not begun to
address the problem spelled out in the protests of the would-be curricula reformers. The history courses taken by future teachers of
American history are the same biased courses with the same biased
content often taught in the same way their present biased college
teachers learned them. Even in colleges and universities that have
undergraduate programs in black studies, where black history or
American history from a black perspective is taught, such courses
are often not listed or cross-listed by the history departments, and
seldom are they developed or offered by or in cooperation with departments of history. If a department of Afro-American studies or black
studies has been developed, the rationale used by other departments,
not including or mentioning black achievements or contributions, is

usually "that falls under black studies, and we have a separate department or program for that." Students who expect to become history
teachers will not meet the requirements of most college history departments or state departments of education for certification by majoring
in black studies. In many instances, black history courses are not
credited toward the history major, thus students taking black history
courses are penalized by being forced to take additional courses in
"white" history in addition to or in spite of ones they might take in
black history. Until history majors are required or allowed to take
black history as an option, a striking educational disability for future
teachers will continue to evolve from this educationally inequitable
process. The ethnocentrism being perpetrated on future teachers
through the perpetuation of such a one-sided view of American history
in colleges has actually resulted in many teachers becoming what C.
Vann Woodward calls historical nationalists. James Baldwin has
summed up the situation, emphasizing the effects and the consequences
on teachers, as well as children, resulting from the way in which
American history is being presented in the colleges and public schools:

> . . . If, for example, one managed to change the curric-
> ulum in all the schools so that Negroes learned more
> about themselves and their real contributions to this cul-
> ture, you would be liberating not only Negroes, you'd be
> liberating white people who know nothing about their own
> history. And the reason is that if you are compelled to
> lie about one aspect of anybody's history, you must lie
> about it all. If you have to lie about my real role here,
> if you have to pretend that I hoed all that cotton just be-
> cause I loved you, then you have done something to your-
> self. You are mad.[2]

Before passing over or dismissing Baldwin's comment as an
overstated emotional reaction, the reader should be informed that an
official administrative agency came to the same conclusion as did
Baldwin after a careful review of the matter of teacher preparation
and textbooks used in the public schools of that state. In the fall of
1970 Ron Edmonds, Assistant Superintendent of the Michigan State
Department of Education, convened a group of Michigan citizens as a
part of the State Department of Education's contractual obligation to
seek the means to improve the quality of its services to urban school
districts. A thirteen-paragraph memorandum formed the basis on
which a Michigan project was begun, one of the objectives being to
promote what the state refers to as "cultural democracy." The con-
cluding paragraph of that memorandum stresses the same point as
Baldwin.

Ethnocentrism is profoundly disrespectful to those who are not "in" but it is also dangerous to its perpetrators as they must obviously accumulate a perception of themselves that bears little resemblance to reality. I need not specify the intellectual, psychological, moral penalties for behavior that is not grounded in reality.[3]

NEED FOR WELL-DEFINED CRITERIA AND STANDARDS FOR MEASURING THE IMPACT AND EFFECTIVENESS OF BLACK STUDIES PROGRAMS

In developing curriculum and teaching objectives for black and ethnic studies programs, teachers and curriculum specialists must keep in mind the reality of America for black and other nonwhite minorities. The political and cultural dominance has resulted in black Americans losing their African identity in a society that has still not recognized them as Americans. Professor W. A. Low has defined the situation as follows:

> Thus, by an acquiesence enforced upon him, the transplanted Negro in continental America was to lose his spiritual and meaningful orientation to Africa, the meaning of old gods and languages, myths, and legends. Whatever meaningful residues of African cultures were to survive, the remnants were to live in remote patterns and problems of anthropology and sociology. They did not survive as vital, cogent forces in the stream of consciousness of Negro history. Africa became irretrievably lost; yet this loss, paradoxically, opened the way through the enforced denial of Africa, for the acceptance of America.
>
> . . . The student of history looks in vain for serious manifestations and expressions of any kind of African Zionism or Pan-Africanism in the history of the American Negro.
>
> The Negro has been too busily engaged in attempts to overcome the ever present ordeal of daily living in America, often literally from hand to mouth, under exacting conditions of slavery or caste, to pursue seriously any movement toward alienism.[4]

The acceptance of American black people is the reality with which ethnic studies programs in public schools must begin. The angry black youngsters in the Harlem elementary schools who did not feel America was their land gave the reason as being "cause you don't do nothing in it." This is clearly a reaction. In cases where Africa was looked upon as an acceptable alternative to American racism, it was more of an escape mechanism where children could be seen to be looking for a way out rather than embracing a philosophy of Pan-Africanism. One youngster in P.S. 197 felt people in Africa would not be jealous like white people in America. However, the resentment expressed towards white people by many black students in the fourth and fifth grades in the Harlem elementary schools is a cause to reconsider the conclusion drawn by Dr. Low in his historical analysis of the black experience.

> . . . The homeland was so completely removed from the day to day meaning and logic of the American experience, that any inclination to refuse the new home carried grave dangers to survival. Therefore, the possibility of the non-acceptance of the new home was rejected, along with Africa. There was simply no other place than the new home for the Negro to turn—unless possibly to a spiritual home in heaven where he could, even as a slave or caste in a Christian society, figuratively lay his burdens down. Herein lies the paradox of the American Negro's life: a historic devotion, allegiance, and loyalty to America in spite of the intense harshness with which he was often treated here.[5]

This may very well have been seen to be the case as late as ten years ago, when the book in which that statement appeared was published. The angry mood of young black Americans today that has resulted in an assertion of African identity can be seen as a form of protest among many black students and, in younger children, it is clearly related to a rejection of the status quo. Clearly, then, the prejudice of black children from lower-income families toward white people in general can be seen as a response to their perception of the inequities and widening gap between affluent white America and their own communities. In advocating the need for a "nation of Negroes," one Harlem fifth grader mentioned Mayor Lindsey, Nixon, and Rockefeller by name, stating they had money and he didn't. One girl in the same class felt black people were called Negroes because white people think they are "stupid." The findings of the Harlem study reveal an obvious need for ethnic studies programs to focus on the development of social and personal attitudes related to perceptions and reactions of young children to cultural and racial differences.

FAILURE AND TERMINATION OF BLACK
STUDIES PROGRAMS

With all of the problems involved in developing effective cultural heritage programs it should not be surprising that the goals of the programs, which were not popular with many "liberal" educators in the first place, were not reached. Part of the problem seems to stem from the fact that the educational purposes of such programs, such as the curriculum for liberation, as defined by black educators such as James Banks, were incapable of being realized in the existing public school systems. Banks defines the goals of a curriculum for liberation as follows:

> A liberation curriculum for blacks and other
> oppressed groups must not only recognize their feelings
> toward self, but must help them clarify their feelings to
> free them from this kind of psychological captivity, and
> to convince them of their value.

An example of a school district that attempted to reach these goals through a program was school district 7, in the Southeast Bronx of New York City.

This district requested and received federal and state funds, close to one million dollars over a three year period to carry out a Black History and Culture Program for the black children in the district, which also has a high Puerto Rican population.

The needs for this program were defined as psychological, economical, and educational. In preparing the proposal for state funding for school year 1971-72, the coordinator of the program stated in the document requesting funds:

> The needs in the community for this program are
> psychological, economical and educational.
> The students of District 7 and people of African
> descent need knowledge and understanding of the African
> heritage and its contribution to other cultures of the
> world. This will aid in enhancing the self-images of stu-
> dents of African descent. With the strengthening of the
> self-images the students are more inclined to be motivated
> to better themselves economically, because they feel
> they have a place in this world.
> Educationally, we will be correcting the miseduca-
> tion of our students in the area of the facts, the deeds,
> the contributions and the impact of Africans and African
> descents on America and world societies.

143

Thus, we will help to reverse pupils' negative self-images, lack of knowledge and appreciation of their heritage, lack of knowledge of the impact of their group members on the making of America.

The objectives were stated as follows:

Primary
To develop with sixth and seventh graders knowledge of Afro-American Culture and History.

To train approximately 18 cluster teachers in techniques and methodology and content of Afro-American Culture and History.

Secondary
To provide a team approach to curriculum development of Afro-American Culture and History.

To provide children with an opportunity to know and appreciate their cultural heritage.

To develop an awareness with students of the impact and contribution of the Afro-American to the American society and world cultures.

The activities were described as follows:

Participants
Students will use audio-visual materials giving information and developing the techniques of deductive reasoning and critical analysis. Six classes in each of eighteen schools will be instructed twice a week by a specially assigned cluster teacher (tax levied funds).

The children will write special reports, make scrapbooks on specific subjects (Black Americans, Africa), interview others to gain information and use resources of the community. They will watch news and special T.V. programs related to the Afro-American experience.

Students will learn about African customs, dress, laws, politics; Black-Americans in the arts, politics, science, education and sociology.

Trips will be taken to various places of educational interest.

Others
Teachers will have grade conferences and individual conferences to learn to develop lessons in Afro-American studies.

Teachers will be observed by the coordinator and teacher-trainer in order to aid them in developing accurate and effective lessons.

Teachers will be offered an in-service course on Black studies.

A general description of the project was presented as follows:

Afro-American Culture and History Program will continue in September 1971 in fourteen elementary schools and four junior high schools. The program will be conducted as an integral part of the history and social science program, during the regular school day.

Materials purchased and developed in this program will be sent to the teachers in the district for use in their social studies lessons. The coordinator assistant coordinator, auxiliary trainer, paraprofessionals of this program will visit teachers in the various schools to offer suggestions for the effective use of those materials. The coordinator will meet with teachers at grade conferences, staff conferences, or at other times convenient for the individual teachers.

A multi-media approach will be employed giving pupils an opportunity to develop the techniques of inquiry and discovery. Rich and varied current materials in Afro-American culture and history will be used to reach the goals of this program (books, records, pictures, slides, filmstrips, etc).

Consultants will be hired to help plan and implement special programs.

In 1972-73, the name of the program was changed from Afro-American Culture and History to the Black Culture and History Program. The planning of the program was broadened as follows:

The planning of this program was done in conjunction and consultation with the Afro-American Culture and History Program's staff, the Advisory Committee, P.A. presidents, parents, Afro-American school coordinators, cluster teachers of Black Studies and the Community School Board.

The program reflects the suggestions of the State Education Department and Mobicentrics, Inc.

Program activities were also modified:

Students will use audio-visual materials gaining
information and developing the techniques of deductive
reasoning and critical analysis.
Six classes in each of nineteen schools will be instructed twice a week (forty-five minute periods) by a
specially assigned Cluster Teacher (tax levied funds). It
is hoped that teachers with background in Black Studies
will volunteer for this position.
The children will write special reports, make
scrapbooks on specific subjects (in Black Studies) and
use resources of the community. They will watch news
and special television programs pertaining to the Black
experience.
Students will learn about African customs, dress,
laws and politics; Black Americans in the Arts, politics,
sciences, education and sociology.
Trips will be taken to various places of educational
interest, such as the Studio Museum, the Schomberg and
Countee Cullen libraries, Helio Museum, Brooklyn
Museum, the Museum of Natural History and Black Expo
1972.

After this program had been in operation for three years, the
New York State Education Department revised its program priorities
for federal and state aid. The new priority emphasis was stated as
being bilingual, mathematics, and/or reading education. In a letter
to all school superintendents in New York City districts receiving
state aid from the Division of Urban Education of the Assistant Com-
missioner's Office for compensatory education, dated February 23,
1973, it was stated that:

The priority emphasis on bilingual, mathematics
and/or reading education necessitates major redirection
and planning of Urban Education projects currently operating in your district.

A list of three categories was defined. Category III, under which
the Black History and Culture Program (as well as seven other programs) was placed, was described as follows:

Each project listed in this category is determined
as unsuitable to affect direct, positive impact on academic
achievement of eligible participants in the priority areas.

146

Therefore, these projects will not be approvable for reimbursement through Urban Education aid in 1973-74. The funds presently being expended to support these projects should be used to expand projects identified in category I or to develop and implement new projects in bilingual, mathematics and/or reading education.

In many situations such as this, the community representatives have stated that the needs and priorities of educational programs should be field-centered and determined by the community, rather than in Washington or Albany. Even if the state's priorities had included Cultural Heritage programs under categories I and II, which were labeled "Direct relationship to priorities" and "Borderline relationship to priorities," respectively, there is no guarantee the programs would have been reimbursed in 1973-74, unless their effectiveness could have been demonstrated. In another paragraph of the letter of June 23rd, the following statement was made;

As previously indicated in Division of Urban Education Program Bulletins 6 (4/71) and 8 (7/71), the intent of Urban Education aid law is to develop more effective and efficient educational practices to replace less effective and efficient practices in the ongoing school curriculum. Therefore, projects listed in categories I and II, which have been operating for two or more years, will require written justification to continue.

The evaluation of the Black Culture Programs funded by state and federal funds was left to outside evaluators who often had less knowledge of the school setting than the district coordinators or teachers. Thus these programs were not only considered weak in relation to mandated priorities, but the lack of a built-in evaluation design further handicapped them in attempting to demonstrate their impact and effectiveness according to uniform standards or objective criteria that the policy-makers would have accepted as evidence.

THE NECESSITY FOR CONSIDERING THE EFFECTS
OF VARIABLES OUTSIDE THE SCHOOL CORRELATED
WITH PREJUDICE AND DEVELOPMENT OF POSITIVE
SELF-IMAGES

At present there is no way of being sure of the degree to which the process of education, that is, ethnic, minority or black studies courses, is related to a lower incidence of prejudice and development of more positive self-image among students taking such courses unless other factors known to be correlated with these two variables, for example, attitudes of family, socio-economic background, reasoning ability, and political orientation are held constant in the analysis.

Obviously the public schools cannot control or influence variables outside of the schools that affect racial attitudes, but they can detect and even measure the extent of such influences. The kinds of information and data obtained from Harlem public schools would be helpful to persons involved in teaching and developing curricula. Schools should be aware of the images and attitudes that most schools claim they are attempting to change or influence. Yet the evaluation techniques of the Harlem schools failed to note the presence, absence, or significance of outside variables when either developing curriculum or attempting to measure the effect of the curriculum on student attitudes. This omission would impose severe limitations on the validity of attempts by researchers to measure the impact or effectiveness of heritage classes or teaching techniques. The validity of any tests to determine the effect of courses in ethnic studies would come into question where children in the same schools but from different social, economic, and cultural settings were compared.

An analysis of the relationship between the effect of ethnic studies programs and other specific dimensions of prejudice is necessary to construct valid assessment instruments. To the extent that a high correlation, negative or positive, can be seen to exist between teaching materials and pride in racial identity in spite of the presence of other variables, for example, low socio-economic status, it might be possible to generalize with some assurance about the effects of ethnic or minority study programs in combating racial prejudice or establishing ethnic identity and pride.

This kind of analysis might also help detect the possible effects of certain outside variables that are not correlated with education but that conceivably interact with education and the way minority children see themselves so as to modify or even force the reconsideration of certain basic assumptions related to developing objectives. For example, it may be that after taking black heritage classes, black children as a group may be shown to be more strongly in favor of African nationalism and perhaps even separatism than those who did not take such courses. However, within the group that took the courses, it may very well turn out that children from lower-class backgrounds would be found more receptive toward separatism than those from middle-class backgrounds, or vice versa.

An effective program in black or ethnic studies cannot be defined by a single set of standards. This study has revealed as many states of educational needs as there are goals and program objectives. Clearly, then, different educational programs under the title of ethnic or black studies will have to be developed to satisfy the needs of different people.

The success of a district or school in developing a program in black or ethnic studies will ultimately be determined by the ability of that school or district to organize a program that makes it possible for individuals to realize their particular or diverse expectations within the same educational setting. This requires the use of plural standards, defining educational needs for different groups and individuals, taking into consideration unique perceptions, outlooks, attitudes, and beliefs, based on different positions and perspectives often within a common social and political system. What is being suggested in personalized rather than individualized instruction, the difference being a recognition of the plurality of ideas and choice by black people in response to oppression, and the departure from a single value system in the former concept.

Evaluations relative to varying definitions of needs must be conducted. The evaluation must be in a large part self-evaluation. In black studies the learners must be made to assume some responsibility for their learning; this means each student should be helped to define and develop a set of expectations as his own reasons for entering a course. In this way, students who choose not to take black studies can be counseled in accordance with their personal attitudes and value orientations. The question is not whether a student needs black or ethnic studies but whether black or ethnic studies are viewed as a means rather than the end. This is a crucial consideration for persons counseling students who are reluctant to enter such courses. Perhaps a modification of the regular school curriculum may be the only way to reach white students and teachers with educational disabilities that have created feelings of insecurity and caused them to aggressively extol or defensively admit their majority membership, Neither condition is conducive to community. Since individual security has its origins in individual identity, and individual identity in America is largely dependent on group identity, perhaps, as an alternative to curricula revision, courses for white ethnic minority students could be developed to help white students and teachers better understand and cope with white cultural defensiveness, which has its origin partly in the untenable task of maintaining the existing cultural autocracy. Today white supremacist views in public schools prevail widely. If there is anything to be concluded from the findings of this study, it is that black studies courses as presently developed in public schools can never be an effective or appropriate response to white racism, or a means of reducing prejudice or discrimination based on white supremacist attitudes.

PROBLEMS IN SELECTING AND CRITIQUEING
INSTRUCTIONAL MATERIALS FOR BLACK STUDIES

Many surveys and studies of what's available to teach the Black
Experience have been so thoroughly undertaken, in spite of the fact
that they have failed to examine the impact of these materials in terms
of their relevance or potential related to the goals or objectives of
black studies courses for black or white students. It would be helpful
for the reader to be aware of the many and elaborate efforts in this
area by several large companies, none of which has undertaken any
systematic survey or research to demonstrate the effectiveness of
learning materials with children.

To elaborate further on this last point, perhaps an examination
of the materials being produced to teach Black Studies and the way they
are selected by educators for use in the classroom would be revealing
to persons concerned with the potential impact of such materials.

The entire Spring and Summer 1970 edition of the Information
Retrieval Center on the Disadvantaged (IRCD) bulletin, a publication
of the Educational Resources Information Center (ERIC) of the U.S.
Office of Education, was devoted to Media for Teaching Afro-American
Studies.[6] This edition reported the results of a media survey to
evaluate the software then available and to report the findings. It was
assumed that this help would serve the educational community as well
as provide the commercial purveyors with guidelines for the preparation of more effective materials.

A discussion of the criticism and praise for materials produced
by sixteen different companies was presented in considerable detail
with a description of the materials. But there was no discussion of
or attempt to predict the impact of these materials.

Black History Books, Black Biography and Autobiography and
What About Us?: How Textbooks Treat Minorities[7] were published by
the Educational Products Information Exchange (EPIE) Institute, a
nonprofit cooperative that conducts studies of learning materials.
These two reports provide descriptive information and commentary
about various types of history textbooks available for teaching black,
ethnic, or minority studies.

The Introduction to Black History Books contains detailed descriptions of over 350 black history books (210 hardcover and 146
paperback), comprising 293 titles. The data were gathered by a
questionnaire developed in consultation with librarians, historians,
and social studies teachers engaged in work in this area and sent out
by the publisher.

This supplement, which is devoted to black history books, also
contains several publications that deal with the historical development
of some aspect of the life and culture of black people in America and

not specifically with matters political or national. Also included is a brief description of the content of each book that the editors describe as suggestive of the scope or special interest of the book but that is not meant to be a comprehensive summary. The editors add that additional information concerning these materials may be secured by writing to the individual publishers and that no endorsement of any product is implied.

The Introduction to Black Biography and Autobiography supplement is devoted entirely to biography, autobiography, and collected biography written exclusively about black people. Listed are books recounting the life stories of persons representing a wide variety of human endeavors and experience, including scientists, politicians, educators, entertainers, explorers, athletes, civil rights leaders, and many others of both recent and past history.

The editors state that this supplement was prepared in response to the growing interest and call for the adoption of black studies materials in the schools, for which a broader, more comprehensive, and descriptive bibliography was needed. To accomplish this goal, EPIE contacted every known publisher of ethnic materials and carefully culled from their literature data on all books in this classification. Supplementary research was then conducted with the publishers' representatives by telephone to secure the additional information felt to be important to educational decision-makers.

In carrying on this research the editors state that every attempt was made to eliminate those books that were either fictional or that gave only partial consideration to Negro figures. As a result, 214 books are listed, comprising 194 different titles by some 69 publishers.

The editors state that the supplement on How Textbooks Treat Minorities, was prepared with the aid of consultants representing various ethnic groups. A questionnaire was distributed to 24 social studies textbooks publishers to determine the extent to which their materials were prepared with the needs of minority groups in mind. A total of 222 questionnaires were mailed, one for each of the textbooks identified in the October 1969 issue of Educational Product Report. Of these, the editors state that 180 or 81 percent replied. What EPIE found was that only eleven, a mere 6.1 percent of these textbooks were written with specific minorities as the intended readers. Eleven addressed themselves to black students; ten of these also included Puerto Ricans; eight, Mexican-Americans; seven, Indians; and six, the children of migrant workers. While not specifically addressing themselves to cultural minorities, a larger proportion (49 textbooks) said they included material illustrative of ethnic groups, and a somewhat smaller number (24 textbooks) included quotations from prominent leaders of these groups.

Again, no attempt was made to examine the reading interests of the groups for whom these materials were intended or the relationship between ethnically related curricula and reading interests.

Perhaps the most comprehensive and recent bibliographic reference on nonprint resources to teach the Black Experience is one produced by R. R. Bowker Company in 1971. This 353-page annotated bibliography of resources contains four position papers related to the special concerns educators teaching the Black Experience must take into consideration. Part Two contains descriptions of the content of multimedia materials on the "culture, heritage, and contributions of Afro-Americans to the growth and development of the United States," and Part Three describes multimedia materials on the peoples of Africa, "their cultures and contributions to mankind." The book is described by its author as a "standard source book" that would greatly assist educators in planning and executing necessary curriculum changes. This reference is the first of its kind for nonprint resources, but there is no attempt to critique or analyze the impact or effectiveness of these materials in terms of what the materials were designed to do or what the courses in which they might be used state as educational goals.

In addition to the materials described above, there are many bibliographies and teaching guides printed by commercial publishers and school districts throughout the United States, but none with hard data of a specifically utilitarian nature that would be of use to program planners concerned with the impact or effectiveness of such materials, based on research or analysis of existing programs. Most either express or reiterate a philosophy aimed at justifying the need for ethnic or black studies at various school levels and make suggestions for topics, themes, learning activities, and lists of materials available for use in the classroom, with no attempt to assess or critique the materials in relation to the objectives of the courses for which they are recommended.

Clearly, then, two points emerge: one, ethnic heritage and black studies programs represent a recent phenomenon about which little of use to program planners and evaluators has yet been written; and two, these programs do represent a rapidly evolving and institutionalizing phenomenon that should be clearly analyzed and assessed, with resultant information made available so that present and future programs may be better developed, implemented, and utilized in and by the school systems, and so professors who will be training teachers for such programs can be kept up to date on all developments. This book has hopefully been a step in that direction, a contribution toward filling a widening gap in information, analysis, and recommendations directed at supervisory personnel, administrators, program planners and evaluators, teacher-trainers, and teachers, as well as decision-makers involved in funding and policy-making for such programs.

NOTES

1. Harry Alleyn Johnson, ed., Multimedia Materials for Afro-American Studies: A Curriculum Orientation and Annotated Bibliography of Resources (New York: R. R. Bowker, 1971), pp. 60-61.

2. Nathan Wright, Jr., ed., What Black Educators Are Saying (New York: Hawthorn Books, 1970), p. 217.

3. 1970-71 Michigan Project, "Improving State Leadership in Education," in Cultural Democracy, a Report of the Members of the Project, July 8, 1970.

4. V. Clift, A. W. Anderson, H. G. Hullfish, eds., Negro Education in America: Its Adequacy, Problems, and Needs (New York: Harper & Row, 1962), pp. 28-29.

5. Ibid.

6. Media for Teaching Afro-American Studies, IRCD Bulletin, vol. VI, nos. 1 and 2. Horace Mann Lincoln Institute, Teachers' College, Columbia University, Spring, Summer, 1970.

7. Black History Books, Black Biography and Autobiography, Educational Product Report, vol. 2, nos. 8 and 9. EPIE Institute, 386 Park Avenue South, New York, New York.

SELECTED BIBLIOGRAPHY

African American Institute. Are You Going to Teach About Africa?
New York: School Services Division, 1970.

Apthaker, Herbert, ed. A Documentary History of the Negro People
in the United States. New York: The Citadel Press, 1969.

Association for the Study of Negro Life and History, Inc. Suggestions
for the Teaching of Negro History. Washington, D.C.: Associated
Publishers, 1969.

Banks, James A. Teaching the Black Experience: Method and Materials. Belmont, California: Fearon Publishers, 1970.

Banks, James A. "Teaching Black Studies for Social Change," Journal
of Afro-American Issues 1, no. 2 (Fall 1972), pp. 141-163.

Black Studies in Schools, Education U.S.A. Special Report. National
School Public Relations Association, 1970.

Breitman, George, ed. Malcolm X on Afro-American History. New
York: Pathfinder Press, 1970.

Breitman, George, ed. Malcolm X Speaks. New York: Grove Press,
1965.

Chambers, Bradford, ed. Chronicles of Black Protest. New York:
Mentor Books, 1968.

Clift, V., A. W. Anderson, H. G. Hullfish, eds. Negro Education in
America: Its Adequacy, Problems, and Needs. New York:
Harper & Row, 1962.

Committe on Labor and Public Welfare United States Senate. Emer-
gency School Aid and Quality Integrated Education Act of 1971,
Report of the S. 1557, Honorable Peter H. Dominick, Chairman.
Washington, D.C.: Government Printing Office, 1971.

Conrad, Earl. The Invention of the Negro. New York: Paul S. Erikson,
1966.

Ethnic Studies in the New York City Public Schools. Bureau of Curriculum Development, Board of Education, City of New York, Project No. 50008, December, 1970.

Franklin, John Hope. From Slavery to Freedom. New York: Alfred A. Knopf, 1956.

Fanon Frantz. The Wretched of the Earth. New York: Grove Press, 1965.

Frazier, E. Franklin. Black Bourgeoisie. New York: The MacMillan Company, 1957.

Harrison, Charles V. "Black History and the Schools," Ebony Magazine, December, 1968, pp. 111-122.

Human Relations Council, Madison Public Schools. Status Report with Recommendations on: Recruiting and Retaining Teachers and Administrators from Minority Groups, 1971.

Johnson, Edwina C. "An Alternative to Miseducation for the Afro-American People," in What Black Educators are Saying. New York: Hawthorn Books, Inc., 1970.

Johnson, Harry Alleyn, ed. Multimedia Materials for Afro-American Studies: A Curriculum Orientation and Annotated Bibliography of Resources. New York: R. R. Bowker, 1971.

Jones, LeRoi. Home. New York: William Morrow, 1969.

Katz, William Loren. Eyewitness: The Negro in American History. New York: Pitman, 1968.

Katz, William Loren. Teacher's Guide to American Negro History. Chicago: Quadrangle Books, 1968.

National Urban League, New York City. "An Analysis of the Implementation of Black Studies Programs in the Public Schools," A proposal submitted to the U.S. Office of Education Research Bureau, Summer, 1970.

Patterson, Dr. Orlando. "Rethinking Black History," Harvard Educational Review 41, no. 3 (August 1971), pp. 297-315.

Quillen, James. "The Evolving Objectives of Education in American Life," The Educational Record 39 (July 1958), p. 222.

155

Silberman, Charles E. Crisis in Black and White. New York: Random House, 1970.

Subcommittee on Labor and Education of the Committee on Education and Labor, House of Representatives, 91st Congress, Second Session, HR 14910. Ethnic Heritage Studies Centers, A Report on the Hearings before the General Subcommittee, February-May 1970, Honorable Roman C. Pucinski, Chairman. Washington, D.C.: Government Printing Office, 1970.

Sweezy, Paul M. "Afterword: The Implications of Community Control," Schools Against Children, ed. Annette T. Rubinstein. New York: Monthly Review Press, 1970.

156

RAYMOND H. GILES, Jr., is Assistant Professor of Education and Chairman of the Department of Afro-American Studies at Smith College.

As Director of In-Service Teacher Education Programs at the African-American Institute from 1967-70, he developed and supervised In-Service Programs for the New York City, Chicago, Philadelphia, and Washington, D. C., school districts. He also led a Summer Study Program for teacher trainers in West Africa in 1969, 1970, and 1971. He has worked extensively in developing teacher training programs throughout the country as well as abroad.

Dr. Giles received his Ed. D. from the University of Massachusetts, his M. A. from Hunter Graduate School of Education, and his B. A. from Hunter College.

RACE MIXING IN THE PUBLIC SCHOOLS
Charles V. Willie
with Jerome Beker

SCHOOL BOARDS AND SCHOOL POLICY:
An Evaluation of Decentralization in New
York City
Marilyn Gittell
with Maurice R. Berube, Boulton H. Demas,
Daniel Flavin, Mark Rosentraub, Adele Spier,
and David Tatge

POLITICAL SOCIALIZATION OF CHICANO
CHILDREN: A Comparative Study with
Anglos in California Schools
F. Chris Garcia

BLACK TEACHERS IN URBAN SCHOOLS:
The Case of Washington, D. C.
Catherine Bodard Silver